Going To The Net

Bill Bishop

ISBN-10: 1499777701
ISBN-13: 978-1499777703

The mind is the forerunner of all things

Siddhartha Gautama

CONTENTS

CHAPTER 1
THE NEW RULE

It was the same old story.

I was up 4-1 in the third and final set. Up to that point, I'd been feeling confident and totally in charge of the match. But as we changed ends, I got a sick sensation in my gut, and a deep fatigue came over me. It was the same feeling I had experienced a thousand times before.

That's when the momentum shifted. I began playing defensively, hitting the ball more cautiously and hoping my opponent would make a mistake. On the other side of the court, with nothing to lose, he took charge. He started hitting harder ground strokes and rushed to the net at every opportunity.

Coming off the court a short time later, I was really angry with myself. I had blown the match, losing the last five games in a row against a weaker player. My opponent had played well, but I had played better, up until the last five games. Right up until it mattered. It was the same old story because it wasn't the first time I had blown it in the final stretch of a match.

At 45 years of age, I had always been a good tennis player. I had played junior tennis tournaments starting at age 10. People thought I had a lot of talent. But I never won a tournament. I was in the finals a few times, and yet I had never won the final match.

At best, I was a perennial runner up.

As I thought back over 35 years of tennis, I felt I had never achieved my full potential as a player. In fact, at age 25, after teaching tennis for five years, I gave up the game completely. I just couldn't handle the frustration. Now, as I was approaching middle age, I had decided to take up tennis again, and perhaps play in some senior tournaments. But I was still confronting the same old problem: I kept losing matches by blowing a lead.

At that moment, sitting by the courts in Palm Springs, California, chugging back a cold bottle of Gatorade, I became convinced the problem wasn't just my tennis game, it was about me and my life. I thought: *Maybe I'm just a second-rate person.* A few years previously, I had gone through a painful divorce. My marketing company was earning me an okay living, but I wasn't rolling in money.

My tennis game seemed like a mirror of my life: I wasn't winning tennis matches, and I wasn't winning at the game of life. *Maybe,* I thought, *I am just a loser, period.*

Fortunately, my despondency and self-doubt were about to end. I didn't know it at the time, but I was at a watershed moment, a turning point in my life and my tennis game.

Later that evening, I had dinner with my girlfriend Ginny. We had been together for a few years, and our relationship was going great. She was the perfect woman for me: smart, kind, and beautiful. There was only one problem. I was worried I would screw up our relationship while things were going well, just like I did on the tennis court.

We had come to the tennis resort in Palm Springs so Ginny, a doctor and psychotherapist, could attend a conference on cognitive-behavioral therapy (CBT), which was a relatively new and increasingly popular way to help people deal with their personal issues. I had decided to come along to play tennis while she attended the conference.

Ginny was very excited about what she was learning about CBT, and had lots of ideas on how the new approach could help her patients. I asked her to explain how CBT worked.

"I could tell you in scientific terms, but to really understand CBT, you need to experience it," Ginny said. "Do you have an issue that keeps coming up in your life?"

My tennis problem came to mind. "Every time I play tennis the same thing happens. When I get ahead in a match, and I'm just about to win, I give up and let the other guy win. This week, I realized I've been doing it all my life."

With a knowing but empathetic look, Ginny said: "I see. So what are you feeling when you get ahead in a match?"

"It happens when I'm a few games away from winning. I get a sick feeling in my stomach and feel really tired."

"When that happens, do any thoughts keep coming up? In CBT, we call them hot thoughts."

I wasn't sure how to answer Ginny's question. I was aware of my physical sensations, but my thoughts were a different matter. I'd never thought about thinking about my thoughts. Then it came to me.

"I know! I think that I'm a bad person, that I'm a bad person for trying to beat the other guy. I guess that's my hot thought."

"Do you really think you're a bad person if you beat your opponent?"

"Not really. I know it's just a game. But it's interesting because even though I know that rationally, I can still feel bad if I try to beat someone."

"That's because you have an underlying assumption that beating someone in a game makes you a bad person."

Feeling a little out of my league in the discussion, I said: "What's an underlying assumption?"

"It's a deeply held, often unconscious conviction or rule that governs how you think and behave. It's a rule that you might not agree with rationally, but you still act on anyway."

"Why is that?

"Because we form these rules during childhood to help us deal with the world around us. This conditioning then governs how we see the world as an adult. For example, you might have formed an underlying assumption that says: 'If I take a chance, I'll get hurt.' So you're ultra-cautious. Or you might have an underlying assumption that says: 'If I try hard, I'll fail and look stupid.' So you don't try hard. Or you have an underlying assumption that says: 'If I trust someone, I'll be betrayed.' So you don't get close to people."

"But how do we form these rules?" I asked, wishing I hadn't

dropped Psychology 101 in college.

"Like I said, it's all about conditioning. When we're young, we experience the world in a certain way. If the environment is dysfunctional, we form rules in order to deal with the situation. Sometimes, we simply absorb the rules being communicated or followed by our parents or other important people in our lives. That's why these rules are often unconscious and not articulated, which is why we usually don't know we're using them."

Ginny's words made a lot of sense. But I still couldn't see where the discussion was headed. I said: "Okay, I think I get that. But how can I deal with my underlying assumption so I can win more tennis matches?"

"We have to come up with a new underlying assumption to replace the old one; a new rule that is more positive. For example, instead of thinking: If I try to win, I am a bad person, you could say: I can try to win, and still be a good person."

"How will that work?"

"The next time you are ahead in a match and you start feeling bad, repeat the phrase: 'I can try to win and still be a good person. I can try to win and still be a good person.'"

For the rest of the evening, I kept thinking about what Ginny had said. I wrote down my new rule, but I wasn't convinced it would work. It seemed too simple. Still, I went to bed that night determined to give it a try.

The next morning was another beautiful day in Palm Springs. Not a cloud in the sky. The perfect temperature. No wind. The pros at the club had set me up to play with a guy named Norm. He was retired and lived in Palm Desert, a sister community right next to Palm Springs. He was one of those guys who play tennis every day. He was 20 years older than me, but looked fit and tough. He had reddish hair, a sunburned face, and muscular arms. He seemed like a good guy.

During the warm-up, I noticed Norm had a consistent strong forehand but a weak, inconsistent backhand. He kept dropping the head of his racquet on his follow-through, sending balls into the net. Because he didn't practice his volley during the warm-up, I also guessed Norm was a baseliner who didn't like coming up to the net.

The game got off to a good start. I was serving well, and hitting my ground strokes with confidence. All the rallies were long, drawn-out affairs, but I was able to win a lot of points when Norm made unforced errors on his backhand. I also hit a lot of drop shots, forcing Norm to the net. I would then pound a passing shot right at him, or lob over his head.

After half an hour, I was up 4-2 and things were looking good, but then the bad feelings started. Sure enough, I felt like a bad person. After all, Norm was older than me. If I kept running him all over the court, he could have a heart attack. Maybe it was mean of me to keep pounding away at his backhand, and hitting drop shots. I thought Norm was a good guy. I wanted him to like me. These thoughts gave me the usual ache in my gut and the deep fatigue. *Here I go again*, I thought.

But then I remembered what Ginny had told me to do. I repeated the new rule under my breath: "I can try to win and be a good person. I can try to win and be a good person." I didn't believe it would work, but I kept saying it anyway.

Guess what happened? It worked. On Norm's serve, I clobbered my returns at his backhand, and kept moving him around the court. I spiced things up with a few drop shots and lobs, and broke his serve at love. At 5-2, I aimed most of my serves at his backhand, and kept him running all over the court.

Norm was getting exhausted. Sweat was pouring down his freckled face. I expected the heart attack at any moment. But I just kept repeating: "I can try to win and be a good person. I can try to win and be a good person." And sure enough, I won the set.

Walking off the court, I didn't feel like a good person, but I didn't feel like a bad person either. I felt kind of neutral, yet also happy that I had won.

Off the court, the power of my new underlying assumption was reinforced when Norm said: "That was a great set. Do you want to play tomorrow?" We then spent an hour sharing stories about our lives, and became fast friends. It seemed obvious that even though I had tried to win, and did win, I was still a good person.

That evening Ginny and I had a drink at a restaurant and watched the sun set over the desert. Excited, I told her all about my match with Norm: "It was great. This underlying assumption thing really works. When I got the bad feeling, I kept saying the new rule, and then I closed out the set."

Impressed that I followed her advice so assiduously, Ginny said: "So what lesson have you learned from this experience?"

"I guess I learned that unconscious rules can sometimes really screw up our lives. That it's important to know what rules we are following because they may be working against our best interests. That seems really obvious with this tennis thing."

"Do you think you've been using this particular rule in your life in general?" Ginny asked, looking very interested.

"I've got a theory," I said, sipping my frosty pina colada. "Maybe I have an underlying assumption that says: 'If I am successful, I will be a bad person.' So even though I work hard and have done well in my career, I've pulled up short because I don't want to become a bad person. Just when I'm about to succeed at something, I sabotage it."

Ginny nodded her head in a way that made me a little uncomfortable. I felt like she was really seeing me for who I was, and it wasn't good. Then she said: "Did this insight teach you anything about tennis?"

"I've learned that I can carry underlying assumptions about my life onto the tennis court: Also, that playing tennis is a way to learn more about myself, and about my life."

"How do you mean?

"I've always thought tennis was separate from my life. I thought it was all about beating the other guy. But now I realize that tennis is a reflection of my life, and by thinking about what's happening on the court, I can learn a lot about my life."

"Do you think you have any other underlying assumptions or unconscious rules that might affect your tennis or your life?"

"Actually, yes. I realize that I operate from the assumption that if I go to the net I will lose the point; that I am no good playing at the net. So for the most part, I just hit from the baseline, and wait until my opponent makes a mistake. I'm afraid to go to the net and take charge of the point."

"Do you think you also apply that rule in your life?"

"Oh yes. I think I'm afraid to engage life fully. I'm scared to take charge and make my life happen. Even though I might put on a big show about being ambitious and all that, when I look at it objectively, there is no doubt that I'm playing life from the baseline. I've got an unwritten rule that I will lose if I go for it. It's like I'm playing my life like a pusher—like a tennis player who just hits the ball back and never goes for it.

"Once again, I can see how my tennis game can teach me something about myself and my life. I just have to be honest with myself about me."

I could tell Ginny was glad I was having these insights. I realized she had been worried about my self-sabotage tendencies. She had also been through a painful divorce, and she didn't want to go through another breakup. Watching the sun fade beneath the horizon, I felt confident that I wouldn't screw up this relationship. I knew I had a lot more to learn, but I believed I had embarked on a journey of self-discovery. I also dreamed about what it would be like to go to the net, both on the court and in my life.

CHAPTER 2
THERE'S ALWAYS A BETTER PLAYER

When I got home from Palm Springs, I signed up for an over-40 tournament at my club. I was ready to try out my new underlying assumption: That I could beat my opponents into submission while still being a good person. What could be better than that? When I looked over the draw, I was convinced I could win. I knew most of the players, and I thought I could beat all of them handily.

I made my way easily through the early rounds, winning each match in straight sets. I was winning and feeling like a good person. It was great! I could feel the trophy in my hands. I could see the adulation of everyone as I stood in the winner's circle. My time had come.

But then in the semi-finals I played Karl, a new member at the club. Even though I'd heard he was a good player, I still assumed I could beat him. After all, I had my underlying assumption thing going for me. Nothing would stand in my way now.

In the match, Karl took the lead immediately by breaking my serve, and he never looked back. Within 40 minutes, I found myself walking off the court after losing 6-0, 6-0. Bagel, bagel! I didn't even get the chance to chant my mantra about trying to win and still being a good person. Karl never gave me a chance.

Crestfallen and discouraged, I drifted home in despair. My new underlying assumption didn't work. Now I would never win a tournament; I would never be number one. Although I loved tennis, I thought about giving up the game altogether. After all, what was the point?

I moped around for a few days, and then came out of my funk. I vowed to soldier on. I decided to look for a new tennis coach, and not just any coach. I wanted to work with someone who understood the technical side of the game, but also appreciated the deeper, more personal issues involved in the sport. I needed someone who understood the underlying assumption game. After asking around and searching on the Internet, I came across someone I thought might fit the bill: Coach Conrad.

Conrad was a former Davis Cup player who had played briefly in the pros before becoming a tennis coach. The biography on his website said Conrad had spent many years travelling in the Far East, and had a philosophical approach to teaching tennis that transcended the basics of strokes and strategies.

Intrigued, I called Conrad and set up a time for a lesson. He told me his first lesson would simply be a conversation. We wouldn't be playing any tennis.

Later that week I met Conrad for our conversation. I was a little nervous because I didn't know what to expect. But his relaxed and affable manner put me at ease. He was about 60 and had sandy blond hair. He looked physically strong. Still, what most impressed me about him was his deep sense of calm. He seemed like an old soul.

"I like to get to know my students before I start teaching them on the court," Conrad said. "I want to find out what they're trying to accomplish by playing tennis. I also have to make sure I want to work with them. I don't take on everyone who asks to be my student."

"What do you mean?" I asked, perplexed and worried.

"I want to know why you play tennis. What are your reasons for playing the game?"

I had never really thought about that before, so I made something up: "I guess I like to compete."

"Why do you like to compete?"

"I want to prove myself by beating the other guy. I want to prove I'm better than the other guy."

"So how is that working out for you?"

"What do you mean?"

"I mean, have you been proving yourself better than the other guy?"

"Not really. That's why I'm frustrated. I thought I was going to win a tournament, and then I lost to a guy named Karl. He slaughtered me. I was hoping you could teach me something that would help me win more big matches, and beat someone like Karl."

"We need to start with your reasons for playing tennis," Conrad said, looking more and more serious. "What do you think you'll accomplish by beating the other guy?"

"It'll prove that I'm better than they are."

"Why do you want to prove that you're better than the other

guy?"

"Well, isn't that the point? I've hit a million tennis balls in my life, and I've hit each ball trying to get to a higher level—to rise above the rest of the players out there. That's why I take lessons and play in tournaments. I'm trying to prove I'm better than everybody else; to be the winner, to get to the top of the heap."

Coach Conrad listened to my rambling answer with a steely reserve. He didn't respond right away, but kept looking at me. I thought my answer was reasonable, though I knew it wasn't the answer Conrad was looking for. I shut up and waited for him to respond. After a long pause, he said: "I call that vertical relating."

"What's that?"

"That's when you look at your relationships with people on a vertical scale. You see people who are below you, and people who are above you. When you use this way of thinking, you're always trying to get higher up on the ladder. This is very common in competitive environments like tennis clubs, but it's also the way most people view all their relationships."

"So what's wrong with that?"

"It's a perfectly natural way to look at things. We all do it sometimes. But it isn't going to make you happy, and it isn't going to help your tennis game."

"Why's that?"

"Because there is always somebody better. You might work really hard to get to the top of the ladder, and think you've got it made, but then someone better comes along. It's inevitable. No matter how good you get, and how many tournaments you win, someone will always come along who is better than you."

"But what about the number one player in the world? No one is better than that person."

"Even the top player in the world is eventually dethroned," Conrad said. "Nobody stays on top forever."

"So what are you saying? Are you saying I shouldn't compete?"

"Not at all. But you have to look at what's driving you to compete. If you play tennis because you want to get to the top, you'll never be happy—because someone will always come along who is better than you."

"I suppose you're right. But what about my club? There's a guy who has won the championship for the last five years."

"But that's just your club. If he plays at the national level, he might not even make it through the first round."

"I see what you mean. No matter how well I do at my club, there is always another level, and then another level after that. I guess I have to give up this fantasy that I'm going to play Wimbledon some day."

"There's nothing wrong with striving to play at the next level. You just have to put things into perspective. Otherwise you will never be completely happy, either in your tennis game, or in your life."

"What do you mean?

"Most people spend their whole lives trying to get ahead of the other guy. Not just in sports. They look at their friends and associates, and see people who they think are below them, and others who they think are above them. They think about their car. It's nicer than Fred's, but not as nice as Stan's. They think about their job. It's better than Susan's, but not as good as Nancy's."

"Is that what you mean by vertical relating?"

"Absolutely. You can see the whole world that way. And if you do, then you'll never be happy, because no matter how hard you strive, there will always be someone out there with a better car or a better job. It's like climbing a ladder that never ends. It just goes up and up."

"So you think I'm doing that with my tennis game?"

"I don't know, what do you think?"

"I think I've been vertical relating in tennis my whole life. Every player I meet, I think about whether I'm better or worse than him. If I think I'm better than him, I get a boost, and if I think I'm not as good, I get a depressed, scared feeling."

"That's your ego talking."

"What do you mean? Are you getting all Freudian on me now?"

"Yes, Freud talked about the ego, but I'm using the term ego in a more general sense. You could also call it the persona or the personality. The ego is the idea we have about ourselves, about who we think we are. The ego is obsessed with vertical relating because it's always trying to define itself. That's the ego's number one job. In order to define itself, it compares itself to others. So it says: 'I'm better than that person and worse than that person. I'm richer than so-and-so and poorer than that other person. I'm better looking than her and uglier than that other woman.'"

"I have to admit, I get caught up in that."

"Don't worry, everyone does it. But if your ego is running your game, you are never going to get better at tennis, and you're never going to be truly happy in your life."

"I'm not sure I understand what you mean by my ego. You make it sound like a separate thing. Isn't my ego really just me?"

"That's a great question. Actually, your ego is a fiction. It's just a package of words and ideas you have about yourself. It isn't real, it's just made up. But we tend to forget that it's a self-made construct, so we think our ego is who we are."

"That's pretty wild. So what are these words and ideas you are talking about?"

"Your ego tells you: 'I'm smart. I'm a good tennis player. I'm successful.' Or 'I'm stupid. I'm a bad tennis player. I'm a failure.' We create these definitions to figure out who we are. But these definitions are created primarily by comparing ourselves to others. We are saying: 'I'm smarter than that guy. I'm a better tennis player than those people. I am less successful than my brother-in-law.' That's why we get so caught up in vertical relating. It's our ego trying to define itself."

"I don't know. I guess you're right. But what's it got to do with tennis?"

"We have a lot more lessons to learn first," he said with a wink. "We can pick up this conversation next week out on the courts."

"So you mean you'll take me on as a student, even though I'm caught up in ego and vertical relating and all that stuff?"

"Absolutely. As long as you have a good attitude and are willing to look honestly at yourself, I think I can help you. See you next week."

CHAPTER 3
IT'S NOT ABOUT HITTING THE BALL HARD

Although tennis was my passion, I also had to make a living. I owned a marketing company. And even though the company was successful, running the business wore me out. I was a classic workaholic. I put in 14-hour days; sometimes working nights and weekends. I thought the only way to succeed was to drive myself and my team to the limit of our endurance.

But one Friday night, after a long work week, I came down with the flu. I had suffered through many colds in my life, but this was something else altogether. I was down for the count. I couldn't lift my head off the pillow for three days. And then, just when I thought I was getting better, I came down with a second strain of flu. It was like getting hit twice in a row with a baseball bat.

To make matters worse, I worried the whole time about my business. I lay in bed fretting that my company would go bankrupt because I wasn't there to man the ship.

It took me three months to recover from this double-bill. Following my initial recovery, it was discovered that I had also contracted pneumonia. I coughed for two months.

Of course, my illness didn't help my tennis game. It was difficult to play at peak performance while hacking and coughing and sneezing. Although one time it did give me an advantage. In one match, I came up to the net while coughing and spewing phlegm like a snorting stallion. My opponent was so totally freaked out by my Tuberculean offense, or perhaps utterly disgusted by it, that he completely fanned on his attempted passing shot.

My three-month illness also depleted my stamina and strength. I lost a lot of muscle mass and endurance. I felt old. I could no longer keep up physically with the younger guys, or even some of the older guys. I huffed and puffed around the court. During extended rallies, I felt dizzy and dazed. My arms were flabby and my shots had lost their zip. My once powerful backhand just fluttered over the net, landing anemically near the service line. My once booming serve floated through the air like a sick butterfly that had lost its way.

Depressed, but not resigned, I took a lesson with Coach Conrad. I hoped he could help me get back my high-voltage ground strokes and my locomotive serve. Determined to show him I was no mini-mouse, I blasted every shot as hard as I could. I wanted Conrad to know that I was a powerhouse, not some lily-laced ball pusher.

After I'd spent about 10 minutes hitting bone-crushing forehands and backhands, Conrad called me to the net.

"How is it going?" he said "I heard you were sick! You okay?"

"Sure, why do you ask?"

"You're really pounding the ball. I was wondering if there is anything wrong."

"No, I feel great. I feel like I'm getting my game back again."

"But do you know that half of your shots were either long,

wide, or in the net?"

"I wasn't really keeping track, but maybe you're right," I said, sensing that Conrad's real lesson was about to begin.

"You know, tennis isn't just about hitting the ball hard. Too many players think that's what they are supposed to do: pound every ball. They watch the pros hit 150-mile-an-hour serves and they think that's how the game is played. But they don't realize the pros can do something they can't do: hit the ball like a cannonball and still get it in."

Standing at the net, puffy-faced and out of breath, I felt confused by Conrad's comment. I had always thought tennis was a power game. You are supposed to hit the ball as hard as possible on every shot. That's what a real player does. My tennis buddies and I had always heaped scorn on the ball-pushers at the club who just tried to keep the ball in play.

"What are you saying?" I asked incredulously. "Are you saying I shouldn't hit it hard?"

"Sometimes it's appropriate to hit the ball hard. If you want to keep your opponent away from the net you might have to hit hard, deep ground strokes. Or you might have to hit a hard passing shot when he comes to the net. But most of the time you have to make sure you place the ball and get it in. There is no point in blasting every shot and hitting two out of three out."

I felt my world crumbling beneath my feet. Conrad was challenging one of the basic cornerstones of my game. If not hard, then what?

"So what should I do differently?" I asked, wishing at this point that I hadn't booked the lesson with Conrad.

"It's about getting the right result, not about power. The goal is to get the result you want, using just the right amount of power, no more, no less. Watch someone like Roger Federer. He hits the ball hard, but he never uses more power than he needs. For example, there are players with faster, harder serves, but Federer usually gets more aces than them. And he knows that an ace at 120 miles per hour is better than an ace at 150 miles per hour."

"I don't get it. Isn't a 150-per-hour serve better? Isn't that why they have those speed guns at tournaments, to see who has the fastest serve?"

"Sure, it's fun to see who has the fastest serve, but it's not the objective of the game. They don't give out trophies for the fastest serve. The objective is to win. Players who use an extra 30 miles per hour they don't need to serve an ace aren't farther ahead. In fact, it's the opposite. They use up their energy faster and wear down their body. That's why some big hitters often make a splash overnight in the pros before suddenly disappearing as quickly as they appeared."

"I'm hearing what you're saying, and it makes sense, but I don't want to turn into a pusher," I said adamantly.

"No one is saying you should push the ball. That's just as bad as blasting every shot. Pushing the ball means you're being too careful and not using enough power. The trick is to use the right amount of power for each particular shot."

I knew Conrad was right. For 35 years, I had been trying to either pepper the ball or play it safe, depending on my mood. I realized that either way wasn't natural, yet I didn't understand why I was doing it.

Conrad could sense I was having an epiphany of sorts.

"It's the ego at work again," he said. "We blast the ball because we want to prove we are stronger and more powerful than the other guy. Or we push the ball because we are afraid of losing and looking bad. Either way, it's the ego defending its turf."

"Can you explain this stuff about the ego again?" I asked.

"Everyone has an ego. It's part of being human. You just have to decide if you want it to play the game for you. When you go out on the court, you actually take two people out there: Your natural self and your ego self."

"You mean I'm really two people?"

"Kind of like that. Our natural self knows what needs to be done to get the desired result. It's not trying to impress anybody or protect anything. It just enjoys the moment and stays focused on the fun of the game.

"On the other hand, the ego is constantly coaching and commenting from the sidelines. Watch the ball. Hit it harder. You idiot. You better not lose. I can't believe you missed that volley. The ego wants to be in charge because it thinks it knows better. It is also very concerned about its image. It wants to be more powerful than the other player. Or it starts pushing the ball because it starts worrying about making a mistake."

"You don't have much good to say about the ego," I said. "Is it really that bad?"

"Like I said during our last lesson, the ego is a false self. Because it's not real, it spends all of its energy trying to prove its existence. It does this by comparing itself to others and by trying to surround itself with possessions and achievements. It also sets the stakes very high. It can make a tennis game into a life or death struggle."

"So how do I know when it's my ego in charge or my natural self?"

"It takes a certain degree of self-awareness, but you start to notice a two-way conversation going on in your head. This is the ego telling you what to do."

"Should I stop listening to my ego?'

"No. At this point, it's insightful to listen to what the ego is telling you. Then you can decide if you want to take orders from your ego and act on them."

"What is my ego telling me to do?"

"Well, you tell me. It's your ego," Conrad said with a grin.

"Well, I guess my ego has been telling me to pound the ball, to show people that I am strong and powerful."

"Do you want to obey that order from your ego?"

"Not really. Obviously if I am hitting two out of three shots out, I'm not going to get the results I want."

"And what are the results you want?"

"I want to win the game and do it with just the right amount of effort and power, no more, no less."

"Okay, so let's play a set and see what happens."

For the next half hour, Conrad and I played a match. My ego was telling me to hit the ball hard and put on a big show, but I decided not to obey. I turned down the power a few notches. I concentrated on hitting the ball deep, rather than just hard. I aimed for wider angles, and spiced up my shots with some spins and drop shots. I threw in a few lobs, and occasionally I decided to hit a surprise cannonball return.

Walking off the court, Conrad asked: "So how was that?

"It was fantastic," I said, beaming. "My ego was jabbering away at me to hit the ball harder, but I didn't obey. On each shot, I focused on getting the result I needed with just the right level of power. It was actually easier."

"That's what people find. When we stop taking orders from our ego, we stop striving so hard. Then we get better results with less effort."

"I know. I played way better and it seemed like less work."

Heading back to the office, I thought about my experience out on the court, and realized I had also been letting my ego run my business. I was trying too hard. I made the whole operation a big struggle. My ego told me that if it wasn't hard, and I wasn't pushing myself to the limit, then I wasn't going to be successful. I had always believed a saying someone told me: "Work is hard, that's why they call it work."

But maybe not. From that day forward, when at work, I made it my intention not to take orders from my ego. I endeavored to get better results with less effort. And just like on the tennis court, it worked.

I spent more time building relationships with my staff and my clients. I focused on the joy of work, rather than just the money. I took my time and paced myself. And I noticed I had more energy at the end of the day, and looked forward to work when I got up in the morning.

Although I occasionally forgot Conrad's lesson and started obeying my ego again, I was able to catch myself at it. Sometimes I would go a whole week, pushing myself and my team, and then wake up and notice what I was doing.

I realized then that this was a practice, more than just a lesson you learn once and apply. You have to keep catching yourself falling back into the ego trance, and put yourself back on the right path.

I also had more fun on the tennis court. I was less concerned about winning or losing, and more interested in the game itself. I noticed how ineffective some of the other players were because they were hitting the ball too hard. I could see that their ego was in charge on the court, and how it was hurting their game. I could also see that they didn't even know they had an ego and that it was running their game, and their life.

A few weeks later, I told Conrad about my new-found approach to tennis and life. He was pleased and happy for me. "You know," he said, "people think the ego is powerful and full of itself, but the opposite is the truth."

"What do you mean?"

"The ego is profoundly insecure. Because it's not real, it doesn't believe in itself. So it does everything it can to prove to the world that it's the best. That's why lots of tennis players hit the ball so hard. They don't really believe in themselves."

"Wow, I never thought about that," I said. "But it all makes sense. People pound the ball because they don't believe in themselves and their abilities. They compensate by hitting every ball like a rocket."

"That's the sad part." Conrad said. "We take orders from the ego without even knowing it. We might not even know we have an ego. We just think the ego is us, and that traps us in our conditioning. For the most part, this conditioning tells us we are inadequate, so we puff ourselves up by hitting the ball hard, or doing a hundred other things to prove ourselves. And if we don't wake up, we spend our whole life marching to our ego, and never get the satisfaction we want."

"So how do we get out of this ego trap?" I asked. "How can we escape from the dictates of our ego? And how can we translate that into better results on the tennis court?"

"Let's leave all that for another lesson," Conrad said.

CHAPTER 4
DON'T LISTEN TO THE STORIES IN YOUR HEAD

I love stories. I've been a voracious reader and movie watcher all my life. I also appreciate anyone who can tell a compelling story, with colorful characters and a plot that pulls you along until a dramatic or comedic twist at the end. But I've learned that not all stories are so wonderful. I've learned that some stories are not worth listening to.

One day around noon, I was waiting for my friend Jason. We had arranged to meet for lunch at a neighborhood restaurant. After 15 minutes, he had not arrived, and I was concerned that he had forgotten our appointment. So I called him on his cell phone. There was no answer and I left a message. After 30 minutes, when he still hadn't arrived, I tried his cell phone again, but still no answer. So I ordered my lunch and ate it in solitude.

Then the stories started. I thought: *Maybe he is mad at me because of what I said about his sister last week. Maybe he doesn't want to see me anymore. Maybe he hates me. He's always been jealous of me. Maybe that's it. Or maybe he got hit by a bus. Maybe he was mugged and is lying in a back alley somewhere bleeding to death. Or maybe he forgot. He never writes anything down. He's so irresponsible. Maybe he's having lunch with someone else.*

Now I was seething. I vowed never to talk to Jason again. He was no longer a friend of mine. But then again, I also felt worried. What if he had been hit by a bus? *Poor Jason,* I thought, *What's going to happen to his family?*

Fortunately, I had a tennis match that afternoon. I knew the excitement of the match would get my mind off Jason. I was slated to play a guy named Max in an over-40 region-wide tournament. I had played him a year earlier and had lost in a third-set tie-breaker. I had felt at the time that I could have beaten him, but I choked in the last few games. I was hoping to redeem myself and exact my revenge this time.

I got off to a poor start in the match. Max took a commanding 4-0 lead in the first set. He was playing solid tennis. He was hitting deep approach shots to the corners and finishing the points with crisp volleys. I was on the defensive, hitting weak groundstrokes off my heels.

But even with this slow start, I was feeling strong and loose. There was no reason why I couldn't make a comeback. Then I started thinking: Max is better than me. I can't beat a guy like him. He's in a higher league. Next I thought: *No it's not him, it's me. I always choke. I'm in a slump. I have a lousy backhand. My best days are behind me. I'm a loser. I'll never be any good.*

Sure enough, it was all true. I lost 6-0, 6-1. I sneaked in a service break in the third game of the second set when Max double faulted twice, and I hit two lucky shots to win the other two points in the game.

Driving home, I kept on thinking: *I don't know why I keep playing tennis. I'm not getting any better. I'm not athletic compared to someone like Max. I should take up curling or darts. Maybe knitting.*

The next weekend, I had a lesson with Coach Conrad. I told him about my game with Max, and the regrettable outcome. I told him all of the things I had been thinking during the game and afterwards.

"You're a writer, aren't you, Bill?" he asked with a little smile.

"That's right."

"So you're good at coming up with stories, right?"

"I hope so."

"Well that's a good thing, but it can also be a bad thing."

"What do you mean?" I asked, leaning against the net post.

"You can get yourself in trouble by listening to the stories in your head. When we play tennis, and something happens that we don't like, we often tell ourselves lots of negative stories. 'I'm not good. I'm in a slump. I can't beat this guy.'"

"That's exactly what I did playing with Max."

"That's right. You start off with one thought, and then follow it with another thought, and in short order it turns into a novel."

"So what's the problem with that? I like stories."

"The problem is that not all stories are true. You don't believe everything you read in the newspaper or see on television, do you? When you watch a movie, you don't believe that it's true, do you?"

"Of course not," I said defensively. "But these are stories I'm telling myself."

"That's the tricky part," Conrad said. "Because you're telling yourself these stories, you tend to believe they are true. And that's dangerous because then you tend to act on them."

"Can you explain that?"

"While you were playing Max, and got behind 3-0, you started to tell yourself a story. The story seemed so real that you believed it. Then you felt bad, lost your motivation, and played even worse. In essence, you started to behave in a manner that was consistent with your story. And then you lost."

"That makes sense. So maybe I should start telling myself positive stories instead."

"That sounds logical, but it doesn't work either. Let's say you are ahead 3-0. You could tell yourself another kind of story, what you would call a positive story: 'I'm really playing well today. I'm a great tennis player. I'm going to wipe him off the court. I'm going to win the tournament and then move into a higher level. It's going to be great holding that trophy.'"

"It sounds good to me," I said, confused. "What's wrong with that kind of story?"

"It doesn't work because it's just another story. Sooner or later, the match will turn around and you'll start to question your positive story. Then you'll boomerang back to the negative story. You'll keep bouncing back and forth between good and bad stories."

"So it's the storytelling that's the problem?"

"Sort of. It's not the kind of story you are telling yourself. It's also not that you should stop telling yourself stories. The problem is listening to the stories."

"Huh? I'm getting a little confused."

"It's a subtle but important point. When you play tennis, your mind will always tell you stories. That's what the mind does. It never stops telling stories. Sometimes they are positive and sometimes they are negative. The trick is to stop listening to the stories, to cut them off before they get rolling along."

"Can you give me an example?"

"Sure. Let's go back to your game with Max. You're down 4-0. Your mind started telling you a story. It said: 'I'm playing terrible today. My backhand sucks. I'm going to lose.'"

"Yup, that's what happened."

"At that point, you had a choice. You could have chosen to listen or not listen to the story."

"How would I do that?"

"You can try what I do. You can simply say to the storyteller in your mind: 'Not right now, thank you. I'm playing tennis.'"

"You tell that to your mind?"

"That's right. You thank your mind for its input, but let it go for now."

"That's interesting. Do you do anything else?"

"You can distract yourself from the story by feeling your feet on the ground and the tennis ball in your hand."

"Do what?"

"Concentrate on how your feet feel on the ground and how the ball feels in your hand."

"What does that do?"

"It puts you into the moment at hand, and helps you drop the story line."

"What happens then?

"It's quite remarkable, actually. If you practice this, you won't follow the story to the bitter end. You won't react to your stories and how they make you feel. You will just concentrate on the game and end up playing your best, moment-to-moment. It doesn't guarantee that you're going to win, but the experience will be much more enjoyable."

"Will the stories ever stop?" I asked hopefully.

"No. Stories are like trains that keep showing up in your mind. But you have a choice. You can either get on the story train, or not get on the train. And eventually, if you stop getting on the train, the volume of stories will drop and they won't take over your game."

I promised Conrad I would take his advice and stop listening to the stories in my head on the tennis court.

The following week I played a ladder match against Mitch, a much younger guy. He had a reputation as a volatile player who was known to throw his racquet while cursing and swearing his way around the court. He was a good player, though, and I knew it would be a tough match.

The game was close, but Mitch got up 4-2. Sure enough, my storyteller sprang into action and started telling me a tale of woe.

I'm going to lose again. Oh no. I'm really in a slump. My knee was also sore and I started thinking that maybe my tennis days were over. Maybe my knee would get worse and worse and I wouldn't be able to play anymore.

But then I remembered Conrad's advice. I said to my mind: *Thanks for your input, but I'm too busy right now to pursue the conversation. I'm playing tennis.* Then I felt my feet on the ground, and also concentrated on the feel of the tennis ball in my hand.

Sure enough, the story stopped. It just vanished like a puff of smoke. Then I got back into the game and won the next six games in a row to win 8 to 4. (The ladder matches are first to eight games, instead of the normal six game sets.)

Looking back over the match, I realized that my storyteller had kept popping up from time to time. When I got ahead, it started saying: *Gawd, you're good. You are playing incredibly well. You are on a real roll.*

Although I liked this story more than the negative ones, I did the same thing. I said to myself: *Thanks for your input, but I'm too busy for a long conversation. I'm playing tennis right now.* I felt my feet on the ground and I felt the ball in my hand.

This experience taught me something very important: When I'm playing tennis, I don't have to get so caught up in my stories. I can let them come and go, without grabbing onto them. I also realized that most of the stories I tell myself are not true. They are not based on reality.

The following week, I got a call from my friend Jason. "Bill, I need to apologize to you. Two days before our lunch, I had to leave the country on short notice. It was a last minute thing, and I totally forgot about our appointment. When I realized it, I couldn't reach you on my cell phone because I was in a remote area with no service. I'm sorry about that."

That's when I realized Conrad's advice about self-storytelling went well beyond just my tennis game. It applied to my whole life. When things happen, I often make up stories about them. But most of the time, my stories are wrong. They are just concoctions invented by my mind to explain the world. They aren't based on reality.

With this insight, I made a decision. I decided to stop believing every story that came into my mind. Now, whenever the storyteller gets going, I simply say: *Thanks for your input, but I'm too busy right now for a story. I've got a life to live.* Then I feel the ground under my feet, take a full breath, and concentrate on what is right in front of me: like a baby, a cat, a project.

This practice has not always been easy. On occasion, I get a story going in my head and ride it for hours, days, even weeks. The longer the story goes on, the more elaborate it becomes, and the more true it seems.

The stories are about almost anything: my business, my friends, my family, and especially about myself. But then I catch myself. *My gawd*, I gasp. *It's another story.* And I am amazed that I hadn't noticed that the story train had been running for weeks. And in that moment, the story no longer has a hold over me. I can decide if I want to keep riding that story train or get off. And most of the time, I can see no value in staying on the train.

I've also became aware of stories I've been telling myself for my entire life. Stories that got started before I could even talk: Stories that were handed down to me from my ancestors. And once again, seeing them as simply stories, I can decide if I want to listen to them, believe them, and act on them. That has been very helpful indeed.

CHAPTER 5
AN UNEXAMINED GAME
IS NOT WORTH PLAYING

In my early 20s, I taught tennis at a ritzy tennis resort in cottage country north of Toronto. It was one of the best experiences of my life. I played tennis for eight hours a day in beautiful surroundings. I met lots of fantastic, interesting people, and I got to play matches against top-notch players from places like California, Australia, South America, Japan, and the U.K. Playing these talented players took my game up many notches. I loved it.

Working at the resort was my first experience teaching tennis. I knew how to play tennis, but teaching it was another matter. To get ready, we were put through a rigorous instructor training program. I learned a lot during those two weeks; mostly I learned humility.

To understand how our students felt, we were required to play tennis with our opposite arm. For me, being a lefty, that meant playing with my right arm. Much to my consternation, I could barely hit the ball. I couldn't hit a forehand, and my serve was atrocious. I felt like a beginner, exactly the effect the instructors were looking for.

I loved teaching tennis. I enjoyed explaining the mechanics of the strokes and the many strategies you could employ. And I found something else even more interesting. I observed that everyone I taught responded differently to the challenge of learning tennis.

Some people were very serious and determined, while others took a relaxed, laissez-faire attitude. Some of my students were very hard on themselves, while others had more compassion for their own shortcomings.

From this experience, I realized you can learn more about someone by teaching them tennis for an hour than you might learn over many years in day-to-day social situations. You learn if someone has a sense of humor about themselves. Whether they are athletic or physically challenged. Whether they are goal-oriented or process-oriented. Whether they are inherently happy or sad, fun or serious. You notice that many students take a more cerebral, analytical approach to learning, while others adopt a more intuitive, learn-by-feeling attitude. I have also observed that some students are tenacious, while others give up easily. Some demonstrate intense energy, while others are downright lazy.

Playing tennis with people reveals a lot about their character. Are they good sports or cry-babies? Are they honest or dishonest with themselves? Do they blame external factors for their shortcomings, or take responsibility and work on them? I've witnessed people slam their racquets on the court and scream obscenities, while others comport themselves with grace and dignity.

I was also intrigued by the impact tennis has on people. There is something about tennis that is so personal. Unlike most other games, except perhaps golf, tennis can really get under your skin. Missing a shot or losing a match can feel like a personal affront to your very being, and hitting a great shot or winning a big match can feel overwhelmingly important. I've seen grown men weep after losing a close match. You don't see that happen when people lose at checkers or even poker, for that matter.

Armed with these insights, and a new-found interest in psychology, I began viewing each lesson as a kind of personality test. This made teaching so much more interesting, and it also improved my instruction. By quickly sizing up my student, I was able to tailor my lessons to suit the individual.

For example, if someone was lazy, I would deliberately hit them lots of drop shots, and get them running from side to side. If they were taking themselves too seriously, I would tell lots of jokes and make fun of myself.

Often, this personalized teaching had hilarious consequences. One woman hit every volley on the wood of her racquet. (Note for younger readers: you might not believe it, but tennis racquets used to be made out of wood). No matter what I told her, she kept hitting her volleys on the wooden edge of her racquet. It was unbelievable. Absolutely every shot. But then I had an idea.

"Why don't you try to hit your volleys on the edge of your racquet?" I suggested. Sure enough, when she tried to do that, she hit her volleys squarely in the middle of the racquet. It was strange, but it worked.

For someone who loved tennis so much, teaching at the resort was like dying and going to heaven. Endless sunny days on the court. Millions of forehands and backhands. I learned a lot about tennis, but the surprising end result was: I learned a lot more about human nature. I became skilled at taking stock of people, and I felt empowered by my new insights. I left the resort feeling more grown up and ready to take on the world. I didn't realize until 25 years later that I had missed one important piece of the puzzle.

***

There I was on the court with Rick. The game started well. I had played Rick dozens of times before. We had always had close matches, but I usually prevailed. In this outing, Rick was leading in the first set three games to two. He was hitting well, especially by running around on his forehand to avoid his much weaker backhand side. I planned to move him around the court to open him up for approach shots to his backhand.

Changing sides on the odd game, Rick was beaming. He had a big grin on his face, and looked like he was having a great time. On the changeover, we exchanged pleasantries and shared a few jokes. It was fun. I was happy to see Rick in a good mood.

Then the clouds rolled in. On his first serve of the next game, Rick double-faulted. I thought, *Well that's a nice little gift*. But Rick was not feeling good about his generosity. He was muttering under his breath, and I noticed a dramatic change in his body language. He looked more tense and stiff.

Sure enough, Rick double-faulted again on the next serve, putting me up 30-love. I could see the anger percolating up in him. I didn't understand the problem. After all, he was ahead in the match, up three to two in games. What was the matter?

On the next point, Rick hit a perfect serve to my front hand side that I could not reach. An ace. I called out to him: "Great serve," hoping that might buoy his spirits a little, which it did. I could see Rick's mood lift and his body relax.

At 15-30, Rick hit another great first serve to my backhand, but I got to it and hit a deep return. During the point, we exchanged more than 20 ground strokes until Rick came to the net on one of my short balls. Taking his approach shot on my backhand, I tried to lob it over his head, but Rick was there for the overhead smash. Reaching into the air, he walloped the ball right into the net. 15-40.

Oh boy. Rick went ballistic. He smashed his racquet to the back of the court. He shouted expletives and railed at the gods themselves. Then he slumped his shoulders and loped back to the service line, where he dejectedly picked up his racquet, and prepared to serve again.

Like the uncoiling of a brown rusty spring, Rick grunted his first serve into the net. More expletives ensued. Then came the second offering: An equally enfeebled, yet enraged service three feet long. It was game for me. Three-all.

On the other side of the net, the reactor rods were heating up. Rick was in full meltdown mode. His perspiration-drenched face raged red. His eyes bulged. I could feel pulsations of radiation all the way over on my side of the court.

From then on, it was an easy game for me. Fully discombobulated, Rick hit more balls wide, deep, and in the net, and the more points he lost, the more unhinged he became. In short order, I won the first set six-three.

In the second set, Rick's mood changed once again. It went from ballistic to fatalistic. Drenched in despair, Rick's body became a loose noodle of nonchalance. He adopted a what-does-it-matter-anyway mien. His attitude was: *What's the point of trying? Life has no meaning, anyway. We're just dust in the wind.*

The air had gone out of his Hindenburg.

I won the second set 6-0. Rick had shown some signs of life in the fifth game, when he got up 40-love, but sank to even deeper depths when I fought back to take the game after a long series of deuce-advantage points.

Slumped, bedraggled, and utterly dejected, Rick proffered a limp, fishy handshake of congratulations, followed by mutterings of reluctant praise for my good play, and the predictable panoply of rationalizations. "I just couldn't hit a backhand today. My serve was off. I had a sore knee."

After trudging back to the clubhouse, Rick then made a hasty exit. "Bye" he flipped back to me over his shoulder as he limped off to lick his wounds, somewhere dark and alone.

Not really understanding this experience, I sat down by myself to cool off and have a little think. I was disappointed in Rick's behavior. He was a good guy, and he obviously had some issues. There were probably things going on in Rick's life that he was bringing out onto the court.

But I was still mad that Rick had essentially given up after losing his serve in the first set. He didn't try very hard after that, and kept throwing away points. I thought: *He didn't try because then he would feel like an even bigger loser. He thought, if I don't try and lose, then I lost because I didn't try. But if I try hard and lose, then I am a real loser.*

Boy oh boy, I thought. *That's screwed up.*

Just then, Coach Conrad ambled into the salon and came straight over to me. "How was your match with Rick?" he asked, taking a seat beside me.

In great detail, I related the whole sorry saga, including the temper tantrums, the flared nostrils, the catapulting racquets, and the ultimate ignominious exit.

"What do you make of that?" I asked Conrad, hoping for some words of wisdom to assuage my lost faith in humanity.

"This is a great lesson for you, Bill," Conrad said. "Rick's suffering can teach you about clinging and aversion. As you explained, Rick was a happy camper when he was ahead in the match at 3-2. His ego liked what was happening. It was clinging to the positive concept of winning. But then Rick double-faulted on the next point. His ego didn't like it. So aversion set in."

Once again, I had no idea what Conrad was talking about, but it sounded interesting. I'd never heard about clinging and aversion before. I asked him to elaborate.

"The ego only has three ways to perceive what is happening in the world: positive, negative, or indifferent," he said. "As we go through our day, our ego judges everything as positive, negative, or unimportant. A cold blast of wind: negative. A friendly face:

positive. A leaf falling from a tree: indifferent. On the tennis court, if we make a good shot, our ego judges it as positive, and if we miss a shot, our ego judges it negative. We can also fall into a neutral stance, where the ego registers indifference."

"But what about clinging and aversion? Where does that come in?"

"That's the trap. When the ego judges something as positive, it clings to that thing and wants it to continue. When the ego judges something as negative, the ego pushes that away with aversion. So the ego bounces back and forth constantly between clinging and aversion. Out on the tennis court, if our ego is in charge, we bounce back and forth constantly between positive and negative, clinging and aversion. Good shot, clinging. Bad shot, aversion. Win game, clinging. Lose game, aversion."

"What about indifference? You mentioned something about being indifferent."

"It sounds like Rick also tried to play the indifference game. After bouncing back and forth between positive and negative, he settled on the third strategy: indifference. He took a who-cares attitude, and then just gave up."

"But isn't this just being human?" I said, scratching my head. "I mean, no one likes missing a shot or losing a game. Isn't it natural to have strong feelings about what happens on the court?"

"Yes, but it doesn't need to be that way. You can liberate yourself from this perpetual cycle of clinging, aversion, and indifference. You can simply watch what is happening in the moment with equanimity—to watch moment by moment your ego's attachment to clinging, aversion, and indifference."

"Wow. Okay. Let's slow down a minute," I said, knowing that Conrad was on to something. "What's this about attachment?"

"The common characteristic of clinging, aversion, and indifference is attachment: being attached to what is happening. That's what the ego does. It gets attached, and then we suffer."

"Well, Rick was certainly suffering."

"That's right. The more Rick became attached to what was happening, the more he suffered. When he was winning, Rick was clinging to the positive. He wanted it to continue. When he was losing, he was clinging to aversion. He wanted it to end. And when he gave up, he was clinging to the notion that it didn't matter anyway."

"So you're saying it was Rick's attachment that was the source of his suffering."

"Exactly. Even though he was in a good mood at the start when he was winning, he was caught up in attachment. That simply set the stage for his counterpoint of aversion. Once that cycle ramped up, it was game over for Rick. He was a slave to both the positive and negative aspects of the game. By clinging, he raised the stakes in the game so high that he lost control of himself. And no matter what happened, good, bad, or indifferent, it wasn't going to help."

"But why did all this attachment business affect Rick's game?"

"Well, Rick was never playing the real game of tennis, he was playing the attachment game instead. He was completely caught up in what had happened in the past, and what might happen in the future. As a result, he was completely unbalanced and out of the moment. When he won a point, he got all puffed up, and when he lost a point, he got all deflated. Playing in this deluded state, he lost any sense of what was really going on. So he couldn't play his best."

"Okay. I don't know if I completely get everything you're saying, but it rings true. I know Rick is a good player, and he beat himself. It is obvious that it was all in his head. So what can someone like Rick, or me, for that matter, do to overcome attachment out on the tennis court?"

After pausing first to choose his words carefully, Conrad began: "It is easy to misinterpret what is happening when you come up against someone like Rick. You might think he was a bad sport. He just doesn't like losing, and when he does lose, he stomps off the court and acts like a jerk."

"Yes, that was my first thought," I said.

"But we can also look at Rick with compassion. Caught in attachment, Rick was suffering. If we consider Rick's suffering from a place of compassion, we can understand his situation much better, and learn more from it."

I had never heard a tennis coach talk about having compassion on the tennis court, but I asked him to go on.

"When we feel compassion for Rick, we see that he has been enslaved by his ego," Conrad said. "It is his ego that is playing. And the ego is never a good tennis player."

"Why not?"

"As I said, the ego is too caught up in the past and future, and in clinging and aversion, to play in the moment. The ego completely distracted the real Rick from his real game. It was unnatural."

"But why should I feel compassion for Rick? Shouldn't I just go for the jugular and take him down? Isn't that the point of the game?"

"Of course, Rick's preoccupations are a great advantage for his opponents. But that is missing a bigger opportunity. If we feel compassion for Rick, we are better able to see his suffering and why it is happening. We can then better see how we ourselves can also become enslaved by our ego and get caught up the cycle of clinging and aversion. Without compassion for Rick, we will never have this kind of clarity, and we will never be able to liberate ourselves from the same problem."

Coach Conrad was making a lot of sense, but it was still hard for me to fully grasp his lesson. "Okay. So you're saying that compassion for the suffering of others will help us end our own suffering."

"Exactly. It is completely in your own self-interest to nurture compassion on the tennis court, and of course in your life. Compassion leads to clarity. Clarity leads to insight. And insight ends suffering."

Thinking later about what Coach Conrad had said, my tennis life up to that point became much clearer. Playing tennis over the next month, I could see how I was caught up in clinging and aversion. My ego judged every shot, every point, every game, as either positive or negative. I wanted the positive to continue and the negative to end. It had seemed so normal, and yet now I could see how counter-productive it was. Caught in attachment, I was suffering unnecessarily. When I lost, I was miserable, and when I won, I was thrilled. My happiness was contingent on everything that happened to me, most of which was out of my control.

Then I thought, *Okay, I understand the problem. But how do people like Rick and me break out of our attachment?* Conrad had talked about compassion, but I needed more information.

Luckily, I had another lesson scheduled with Coach Conrad.

CHAPTER 6
YOU ARE NOT WHO YOU THINK YOU ARE

Over the next two weeks, I played several matches in the club ladder. I tried to feel compassion for myself whenever I noticed my clinging and aversion. I found it hard to feel compassion for my opponents, though. Especially one guy named Byron, who acted like a complete imbecile on the court. Every time I played him, he questioned my calls repeatedly, and when he lost, he barked profanities and threw his racquet. I guess that's why I beat him 6-0, 6-0. No, my level of compassion did not yet extend to the likes of Byron. But I did recognize that Byron had lots of personal issues that weren't limited to the confines of the court.

I didn't really get how feeling compassion, and understanding the dynamics of clinging and aversion, could make me a better tennis player. I just wanted to win more matches. *What's the trick,* I wondered.

After the calamitous match with Byron, I had to play Mitchell, a good friend of mine. I always beat him, but we had a great time together, so I liked playing him.

It was a spectacular spring morning when we arrived at the courts. The clay was still dewy, and the city was just waking up. The only sound in the park was the crack of tennis balls as we traded groundstrokes.

After a short warm-up, I started the match on serve, which I won handily. After changing ends, Mitchell won his first serve by rushing the net and hitting a perfect forehand volley out of my reach. On his second serve, Mitchell came to the net again, and I tried to hit a passing shot to his backhand, but he picked it off again, 30-love for him.

At that point, I decided to do something different. When Mitchell rushed the net on his third serve, I popped up a lob over his head. Surprised, Mitchell ran to the back of the court, while I moved up to the net. This turnaround made him so perturbed, Mitchell fanned on his backhand, and I won the point.

That's when I knew I had a winning strategy. When he comes to the net, lob over his head. Don't try to pass him.

For the rest of the match, Mitchell came to the net over and over again. Not just on his serve, but on most points, even when I was serving. And I just kept lobbing it over his head. He would rush and I would lob. This went on for the entire match, and I won 6-4, 6-2. Fortunately, Mitchell was no Byron. He was a good sport.

"That was a great match," he said, with a friendly pat on my back. "Maybe I'll get you next time."

Later that day, I thought about Mitchell and all our games together, going back 10 years. I realized at that moment that Mitchell had been using the same strategy for the whole decade. He would come to the net, and I would lob over his head. For the last 10 years!

That's why he never beats me, I thought. *He keeps using a losing strategy year after year.*

This absolutely astounded me. You'd think he would change his strategy when it didn't work. Why didn't he try something else? But no, he never did, and I suspected he never would.

The next day before my lesson, I told Coach Conrad about Mitchell and his 10-year losing streak: "I don't get it, he just keeps doing the same thing over and over. It's driving me crazy thinking about it—10 years!"

"That's a very common problem," Conrad said. "Most people never change their ways, both on the tennis court and in their life. Even if they are using a losing strategy, they just keep doing it."

"But why is that? Don't they see what's happening? Don't they see that what they're doing isn't working?"

"Sometimes people change their ways, but it's only after something really bad happens. They stop driving recklessly after they have an accident, or they start exercising after they have a heart attack. But most of the time, the consequences are not that severe, so they never learn their lesson. That happens a lot on the tennis court."

"What do you mean?"

"Well, the majority of tennis players never change their losing habits because the consequences are not that bad. It just means they lose a match. It's not a life-threatening outcome. So they just keep going along doing the same old thing, even when it doesn't work."

"But don't they want to get better at the game?"

"Certainly. But they try to do it by practicing more, and playing more matches. We've also seen how some people try to get better by hitting the ball harder, but that doesn't usually work because they aren't learning the lessons they need to learn."

"Does this have anything to do with the clinging and aversion we talked about last time?" I asked.

"Yes it does."

"That's good because I've been a little confused since our last lesson. I still don't understand how being aware of clinging and aversion can help someone become a better tennis player."

"Actually, it's very hard to make real, sustainable improvements to your tennis game if you're not aware of your clinging and aversion. Because if you're not aware of your attachments, then you cling to a fixed idea of self."

"What do you mean by that?"

"Well, the ego is actually an idea, or package of ideas, we have about ourselves. When it comes to tennis, we might have an idea that we're a good player at the baseline and a bad player at the net. Or we might think we are too slow, or too clumsy. Or we might think we have a weak second serve, or that we always choke on big points. Over the years, this idea of self becomes very rigid and hard-wired in our mind. In fact, our brain actually organizes itself around these ideas."

"Tell me about that. About the brain."

"Scientists have discovered that the brain is very flexible. They call this neuroplasticity. Like plastic, the brain can rewire itself. That's a good thing. It gives us the ability to radically change how we see the world and ourselves as we experience new things."

"Wow, I thought your brain was kind of set in stone. That it never changes."

"That's what most people think, and that's how they get stuck. If we do nothing different, our neuro-pathways become more set in stone, like a small path that eventually becomes a superhighway. That's why many older people get set in their ways. Their thoughts and habits have created a certain kind of brain, and in their old age it's hard for them to change their thoughts and habits. But if you make an effort to change your thoughts and behaviors, you can actually change your brain."

"I guess that's one reason why it's easier to teach kids to play tennis than adults," I said. "Their brains haven't been fully wired."

"Exactly. It's harder for adults to learn almost anything, like a new language or new technology. Kids take to new things like fish to water. With adults it's much harder."

"That's interesting. Maybe that's why Mitchell keeps playing the same losing strategy. His brain is rigidly wired and he can't break out of it."

"The good news is that he can break out of it. But he has to be aware of the problem. He has to become aware he's losing tennis matches with you because he's stuck using the same losing strategy over and over again. That's the first step. Second, he has to realize he's using the same strategy because his brain is hardwired around that strategy. And third, he needs to know his brain is hardwired because he's clinging to a fixed idea of himself."

"What happens if he realizes his fixed idea of himself is not who he really is? Does that mean he is nobody, a nothing?"

"That's when it gets interesting. If Mitchell realizes he's fixed on a fictional idea of who he is, then he has the chance to become who he really is."

"Who is he?"

"Well, he's not actually a person named Mitchell. That's just a name his parents gave him. And he's not actually a person with a weak backhand. That's just an idea he made up for himself. And he's not someone with a weak serve. Once again, that's just an idea he got about himself because he double faulted a lot in the past. It doesn't mean it's who he is, or who he might be."

"I think I'm getting this. If Mitchell creates this character about himself in his mind, then he starts to act and behave like that character. Eventually he starts to believe that's who he is, and his brain becomes hardwired around that idea."

"That's right. But, like you said, it's just an idea."

"And if he believes that's who he is, then he keeps fulfilling that role. If he thinks he is someone who misses a lot of backhands, then he will probably miss a lot of backhands."

"Right again. And then his brain starts to wire itself around these ideas, and he becomes more convinced of all these things about himself."

"And if he's convinced about these things, then there's little hope that he'll be able to change or improve his game."

"Bingo. You hit the nail on the head. If you have a fixed idea of self, then it is almost impossible for you to change or improve as a tennis player, or as a person. You're stuck forever in the same place."

"That sounds horrible."

"Well, not to sound too melodramatic, but it's kind of a living death. It's like you become a statue, rather than a living and breathing organism that is constantly changing."

"And if you're a statue, then you're fixed in one place forever."

"Yes. Once people have developed their personality around a certain set of ideas, it can be very hard to change. There's a story about a tiger that shows how hard it is to change.

"Back in the '60s, there was this white tiger named Mohini who lived at the zoo in Washington, D.C. For many years, he was confined to a very small cage, about 12 feet by 12 feet. With nothing else to do, Mohini would pace back and forth in this tiny enclosure. Naturally, many people at the zoo felt bad about this situation, and wanted to do something about it. So they raised millions of dollars and built a new space for Mohini. It was a good acre in size, with a pond, hills, and trees.

"When the day came, and they released Mohini into this new larger space, everyone expected him to be happy and free, to go leaping about in great joy. But that's not what happened. Instead, Mohini starting pacing in a circle 12 feet by 12 feet. And for the rest of his life, that's what Mohini did; he kept within that 12 by 12 foot space."

"That's so sad. But why did he do that?"

"Because Mohini had been conditioned over all those years of living in a small cage. From continuous repetition and habit, Mohini's brain had become hardwired to stay within those narrow parameters. And even though he now had a much larger space to roam, he didn't take advantage of it."

"So how does that apply to tennis?"

"It's the same thing. The longer we hold certain ideas about ourselves, and the longer we play tennis in a certain way, the more hardwired our brain becomes around those thoughts and habits. After a while, if we don't do something about it, we become stuck in a certain way of seeing and behaving in the world."

"So what's the answer?"

"You have to start by understanding what it means to have a fixed idea of self. It's the only way you'll ever be able to make a significant improvement in your game. Otherwise, you will remain a child chasing toys."

"What do you mean by that: a child chasing toys?"

"That's what the next lesson is all about."

CHAPTER 7
CHASING TOYS

Two weeks later, I met up with Coach Conrad. The more I got to know him, the more I noticed that he had a tremendous presence about him. Nothing seemed to faze him. He was like a mountain in a hurricane. No matter what happened on the court, he remained calm and focused. So I asked him about it.

"How do you stay so calm all the time? It's like nothing bothers you."

"Well, thanks for saying that. I'm not sure it's true, but I've worked at it for a long time."

"Worked at what?"

"Well, many years ago, I decided to stop chasing toys."

"What do you mean by that?"

"Well, let's think about the ego, or the mind, if you prefer, as a young child. Like any young child, it likes to play with toys. It likes chasing toys because it thinks they will make it happy. A real child can have a lot of toys, but they are limited by time and space, and the parent's budget. But with the mind, the number of toys is unlimited, and they come in all shapes and sizes."

"Like what?"

"We have actual toys, like cars, boats, or houses. Not to mention gadgets, clothes, and jewelry. Our economy is designed to provide us with these toys. Advertising is aimed at showing us new toys to chase. But it goes beyond physical objects. A toy might be the idea of winning a tennis tournament, or getting a promotion. It might be to seek revenge on someone you dislike, or spread gossip about someone. It might be about improving your appearance, or renovating your backyard. It might as simple as getting through an intersection before the light turns red. These are all toys. And the mind serves them up one after another."

"So what's wrong with wanting all of these things? Isn't it a good thing to strive to get things, and achieve goals? Isn't that what we are supposed to do?"

"We have been raised to think that way. The whole culture is telling us to do that. The problem is that these toys never actually make us happy. We buy a new watch because we think it will make us happy, and then a month later it is just a watch on your wrist. And five years later it breaks or you get bored of it, and then buy another watch. Whatever initial happiness it gave you didn't last very long."

"Are you telling me I shouldn't buy a new watch?"

"No, not at all. But you shouldn't expect it to make you happy."

"But it would make me happy."

"Only for a very short time. It would give you a quick boost of happiness, and then that would fade away. You would soon start looking for another toy to make you happy. And then another toy. You get into an endless cycle of chasing toys, and yet never achieve real happiness."

I had to admit Conrad was right. I had a closet full of stuff that I thought would make me happy, which never did, except for a fleeting moment. "But what about winning a tennis tournament. Wouldn't that make me happy?"

"That would be a great thing, but the happiness won't last. It might actually make you depressed; you could fall into a post-victory depression. That's what happens to a lot of athletes who win a gold medal. They spend years striving for the goal, and then attain it. And then afterwards they fall into a depression."

"So you're saying, don't try to win a gold medal?"

"No, winning a gold medal is wonderful, as long as you do it for the right reasons, and not because you think it will make you happy."

"Why don't these things, toys you call them, make you happy?"

"Because like all things, they are impermanent, meaning they don't last. The illusion we all have is that these toys will give us a permanent feeling of happiness. But because they are impermanent, the happiness they bring us doesn't last."

"So what if you have a new car that lasts for 50 years because you really take care of it? Wouldn't that give you 50 years of happiness?"

"That's a good example. You see, it isn't the car that gives us happiness, it is the idea of the car. And that's where this gets really interesting. When you buy something like a car, you are actually buying into an idea, not just the car. You are buying the idea of what it will be like to drive the car, and perhaps what you will look like in the car. Lots and lots of ideas."

"I get that. So what's wrong with these ideas?"

"Well, ideas are impermanent. For example, you might fall instantly in love with someone. But usually, because you don't really know the person that well, you fall in love with your idea of them. You idealize them. Psychologists call this your 'Imago' which comes from the Latin word for 'image.'

"Eventually, this idea fades away and is replaced by a more realistic view of the person. And then, sometimes, you are no longer in love with them because the original idea, the Imago, is no longer there. So that could happen with the car too. Whatever original idea you had about the car might only last a short time, even if you own it for 50 years."

"Sadly, yes, I've experienced things like that."

"So that is a perfect example. Ideas are very impermanent. They are either dispatched by the light of day, or are replaced by other ideas. And typically, we are most enamored with new ideas, so we are always coming up with new ones to replace the old ones. That's why our minds are so busy."

"Busy chasing new toys."

"That's right. Our mind is constantly spewing up new ideas. It is like a gushing oil rig. We really can't do very much to stop it. But we can stop chasing these ideas."

"So the goal is not to stop the gusher of ideas?"

"Yes, you can't try to stop the gusher because then you would be chasing another toy, the idea of stopping the gusher."

"Wow, that's really screwed up."

"Yes, but it is not uncommon to try and stop it, and build up an idea of yourself as someone who can 'control' their thoughts. That's not what I'm talking about here."

"Okay, so as far as tennis goes, you're saying that when we are playing tennis, ideas are constantly popping into our heads?"

"That's right. As the game progresses, our mind just keeps churning up ideas, and we start chasing them. We think they are real. We have the delusion that they represent something real about us or our situation. But they are just ideas. If we can see this, really see this, then we have a choice. We can either chase them, or we can let them be, and they quickly evaporate."

"They evaporate?"

"That's the interesting thing. If you don't chase after these ideas, or cling to them, they quickly evaporate because they were made out of nothing. It was only clinging to them that made them seem real and permanent, that they were the truth. And if you don't cling to them, you realize they are just like clouds passing overhead. Here one minute, gone the next. Like a flash of lightning, or dew in the morning."

"So how do I stop clinging to all these ideas when I'm playing tennis?"

"Well, there is another character: The mother. There is a mother watching the child chase the toys."

"Who is the mother?"

"That is your authentic self, the one with the wisdom."

"So I'm watching myself?"

"You are the mother watching the child chasing the toys. If you are mindful, you can see what your mind is doing. You can calmly watch your mind clinging and chasing after thoughts and ideas."

"How do I do that?"

"First, it's helpful to realize you are actually the mother and not the child. The child is just your fictional self or ego. It is your fictional ego that is chasing the toys. That's what it is designed to do because the clinging and chasing helps the ego define itself. But the mother—or father, if you prefer—can see what the child is doing. It can see the child chasing the toys, and can calmly decide if the toys are okay or if they are dangerous. Then the mother can intervene, and steer the child away from the toy.

"So if you have this perspective, you don't become lost in your thoughts and feelings; you realize they are just toys. And your mother can help you decide if you really want to chase that toy or not."

"Okay, so take me back to tennis again. How is this helpful?"

"When you are playing tennis, your mind will come up with a lot of ideas. I'm playing great today. I suck. I am going to lose. My backhand is terrible. I should give up playing tennis. I'm invincible.

"If you cling to these ideas, you will be lost in your head. You won't be in your body. You won't be in the game. So your game will be affected. You won't be able to play to your full potential because you are so busy trying to reinforce this idea or that idea. But if you watch your mind coming up with these ideas, as if you are a spectator watching from the outside, you will see the ideas for what they are, just passing fictions. You will then have a choice as to whether you want to keep chasing those ideas. And if you practice this, you will keep catching yourself chasing these toys, and then stop doing it because you will know deep down that they are not real, and that they are not helpful. You will wake up."

"What do you mean by wake up?"

"When you are chasing these toys, you are in a delusion, and the mother is asleep. The child is just running around all over the place. But then the mother wakes up, and it all just goes poof. So that's the practice, you just keep waking up. And eventually, perhaps, you never fall asleep. The mother is always awake."

"Conrad, you are really blowing my mind. I love it. But what about a good idea, like I'm invincible? Isn't it helpful to think that, to think positively about yourself when you are playing tennis? That's what everyone says you should do, keep a positive attitude."

"It sounds good, but it doesn't work. The more you chase the idea that you are invincible, to prop up your ego, the more you will actually convince yourself you aren't invincible."

"Why is that?"

"Well, look at it this way. If you need to get yourself pumped up by telling yourself you are great, the more you realize deep down that you aren't great. I mean, if you are really great, why do you need to pump yourself up? Only someone who thinks they aren't great needs to pump themselves with affirmations that they are great. And you can kid yourself all you want, but your authentic self, the mother, knows what the truth is."

"I've never thought about it that way before."

"That's why most self-help programs don't actually work, especially the high-powered motivational programs. They give you tools to pump yourself up. But eventually you get so pumped up, the bubble bursts, and you are back to feeling deflated. These programs just give you more toys to chase. But they are not sustainable."

"So what happens if I stop chasing all of these toys?"

"Then you will be left with who you really are."

"Well, who am I?"

"I think we'd better leave that for the next lesson."

CHAPTER 8
THE WINCHESTER HOUSE

For the next few weeks, I tried to watch my clinging and aversion while playing tennis. Coach Conrad had instructed me to watch my thoughts after every point. What was I thinking? How was I feeling? What stories was I telling myself?

It was a fascinating exercise. The first thing I noticed was that I kept forgetting to do the exercise. I would get so caught up in the game that I wouldn't even try to watch my thoughts. There was so much going on.

But when I did remember the exercise, I could see I had built up a whole train of thoughts. Sometimes I would play a whole set, or a whole match, without remembering to watch my thoughts. Then I would be hard on myself. I would berate myself for not remembering to watch my thoughts. Then I'd recall Coach Conrad's instructions: "Don't judge yourself for not watching your thoughts. It's okay. You'll get better at it. Think of it as learning a whole new game."

During my next lesson with Coach Conrad, I told him all about my experience: "It was quite revealing. I could see how I would get on a train of thought, either good or bad. If I was playing well, I would want it to continue, and I would try to cling to the idea that I was a good tennis player, and that I was going to win. Or I would go in the opposite direction, and think that I sucked and that I was going to lose. Sometimes I veered back and forth between these two thoughts in a single game."

"Did you have any overall insight about the experience?" he asked me.

"I can see how chasing all of these thoughts makes me a bit cuckoo. I was just making it all up in my head, and I believed these thoughts were real. I could also see how I was totally lost in these thoughts. That they and myself seemed merged together. But when I stepped back, I could see they were just thoughts, nothing more. As you say, the mother could see the child playing with the toys."

"Did the exercise help your tennis game?"

"I'm not sure. I'm not sure I won more matches or anything. But I did notice I was enjoying myself more. I wasn't as attached to winning or losing. And many times, I felt more in the groove. I felt more relaxed and natural, so that's good."

"Anything else?"

"Well, I could really see the clinging and aversion of my opponents. If they made a great shot, they had a look of elation, but if they missed one, they acted frustrated or depressed. I played one guy who got really upset with his game, even when he was beating me 4-0. He missed an easy one at the net, and blew a gasket. I couldn't believe it because he was so far in the lead. I mean, what did he want, to win every point?"

"It sounds like he was building his Winchester House."

"What's that?

"Years ago I taught tennis at a resort near Palo Alto in

California, and I visited this tourist attraction called The Winchester House. It was originally owned by Sarah Winchester, the wife of the guy who invented the Winchester rifle. When he died, she visited a psychic who told her she needed to build a house for herself and for the spirits of the people who had died because of the Winchester rifle. She told Sarah that she would live forever if she kept building the house, and would die immediately if she stopped. So Sarah had people continually working on the 160-room house for almost 40 years until she died in 1922."

"That's one heck of a reno."

"It's an amazing house to visit because there are all of these staircases that lead nowhere, and rooms that are closed off, and all kinds of other wacky things."

"So what does this house have to do with tennis?"

"All of the ideas we create in our minds are part of a much bigger project. When we miss a point, we might get the idea that we have a weak forehand, or that we choke on big points. We cling to that idea. And we also add that idea to a much bigger idea about our tennis abilities in general. Then we add them to the idea that we are a B player and will never be an A player. We start building a whole structure of self around these ideas."

"I get what you mean. These ideas we conjure up are not isolated. They are part of a much bigger whole."

"That's right. And then we add all of our tennis ideas to the even bigger structure of self that we are building, the bigger ego structure we are building about who we are. If we are caught up in clinging and aversion on the tennis court, we are also doing it in all facets of our life. We are building this big ego structure about how we look, about our jobs, about our relationships, and about what we own or don't own."

"I can see what you are talking about. I've been building that structure all my life."

"That's why tennis gets under people's skin. What happens on the tennis court seems so important because it's linked to the rest of our ego structure. If we lose a tennis match, it can affect how we feel about ourselves on a fundamental level."

"Does tennis have that effect on people more than other games?"

"Lot of games affect people's egos, but tennis is one of the most powerful games for a number of reasons. One, when you play tennis, you are on display for everyone to see you. It's like you are naked out there. And people like to watch other people play tennis, so you know people are watching. Two, tennis is a hard game to master, so you make lots of mistakes. And three, there are no ties in tennis. You either win or lose. And in a tournament, everyone goes away a loser, except the champion. That is pretty hard to take for a lot of us."

"I've really noticed that. Many people take tennis very seriously."

"That's because tennis is one of the rooms in their Winchester House."

"Tell me more about that."

"I use that analogy because of something the psychic told Sarah Winchester. She said she would live forever if she kept building the house, and would die immediately if she stopped building it."

"How does that relate to what we are talking about?"

"The ego wants you to keep building its house. It doesn't want you to stop, because if you do, it will cease to exist. So the ego does everything to convince you to keep building. It tells you that you will die if you stop building your house. But the only thing that will die will be the ego, not you."

"How does that relate to tennis?"

"The ego is trying to convince you to keep building ideas about yourself and your tennis game. The ego says you need to be constantly creating your 'tennis-self,' or you will never become a great tennis player. So you start to believe that letting go of your ego will mean you will no longer be able to play tennis. But, of course, the opposite is true."

"What is true?"

"If you let go of your ego and the house you are building, you will probably play a lot better because your thoughts and feelings won't get in the way. You will play with a much more natural flow."

"So you will play better and win more matches."

"Maybe. But you will realize that winning and losing is the ego's limited, very small way of looking at tennis."

"What do you mean by limited, small way?"

"Playing tennis presents an opportunity to transcend your ego, which is making you unhappy. Tennis gives you a forum to see what your ego is up to, and then wake up to the truth that you are not your ego, that you are not your tennis game, that you are not all of the things you own, or the way you look, or the money you have in the bank."

"So I can use tennis as a way to discover who I really am."

"That's right. Think of it as a grand experiment. A laboratory of life, if you will."

"Wow, that's pretty heavy."

"You have a choice. You can let your ego run your tennis game, and your life, or you can free yourself from its grip. You can either continue to suffer, or you can achieve real, lasting happiness."

"That would be great. I'm all for it. So what's the next step? Where do we go from here?"

"The next step is to see the connection between our thoughts and our actions—to see what impact clinging and aversion have on how we behave on the tennis court."

"Why is that the next step?"

"Because ultimately, all of this clinging affects what we do in the world, and this includes how well we play tennis, and how we comport ourselves on the tennis court."

"Okay, so what should I do?"

"Just be aware of how you behave on the tennis court—what you do and what you say. And take note of what your opponents say and what they do."

CHAPTER 9
THE PRE-EXCUSE

With the coming of cold weather, a big, white plastic bubble was erected over the four courts at my tennis club. Truth be told, I always looked forward to the "indoor" tennis season. Playing under the bubble meant no rain-outs, no wind, no sun glare, or other distracting weather conditions. For me, being a Canadian, tennis was actually more of a winter sport than a summer sport.

The tennis bubble season was also time to play in the club tennis ladder. I loved playing in the ladder because I got to meet lots of new people to play with, and I got to play more matches. I had "won" the ladder many times, but my real goal was to stay in the top box as long as I could. At this point, I had been in the top box for five years.

Of course, after my many enlightening lessons with Coach Conrad, I realized I was clinging to this goal of staying in the top box. I was really attached to the idea of staying on top; I was clinging to it. It was a bit of an obsession. I was obviously building an ego house with a room that said: "I am in the top box in the tennis ladder at my club."

Looked at in this way, it seemed kind of pathetic. After all, if better players entered the ladder, I could actually improve my game but end up in the second box. I wondered if that would make me feel better or worse. And what would happen when I inevitably fell down into the second box? How would I feel about myself then? All of this left me a little confused but still excited about the ladder.

My first ladder match was against Troy. He was a tall, bean pole of a guy, about 40 years old. I had never met him before. Troy sauntered onto the court lugging four racquets. Opponents carrying more than two racquets always gave me a little bit of a fright. I figured the more racquets your opponent had, the better he was, but I had also learned that sometimes people carry around a bunch of racquets just to look cool. So I calmed down.

I also noticed he had a bandage on his knee, and before we went out on the court, he told me he hadn't played in a month due to a knee injury. He wasn't sure how well he would play. "I don't think my knee is 100 per cent yet," he said.

During the match, Troy didn't show any signs of disability in his knee. He had a solid game, moved well side to side, and came confidently to the net on his approach shots. But I was on top of my game that day, and won the match 8-3 in less than an hour.

Watching my thoughts and feelings, I realized I felt a little guilty about beating Troy. After all, he had a bad knee. But I was also confused. It didn't look like he had a bad knee when he was playing.

After the match, Troy was gracious in defeat, but then said: "Yeah, my knee wasn't really 100 per cent. I'm sure I would have played better if it wasn't for my knee."

I could see Troy's point. I guess I had only beaten him because he had a bad knee. *If he was 100 per cent, he probably would have beaten me*, I thought to myself.

The next day, I told Coach Conrad the story about my match with Troy. I told him about Troy's bad knee, and why it was the only reason I beat him.

Coach Conrad was surprisingly frank: "That's a bunch of BS. You beat Troy fair and square. It's got nothing to do with his knee."

"You think so?"

"It's the oldest trick in the book. It's called the pre-excuse."

"What's that?"

"That's when you come out on the court armed with your pre-excuse. Your opponent says they have a bad knee, or a hangover, or that they didn't sleep very well. They say they haven't played in two months, or that they are trying out a new racquet. There are a million pre-excuses."

"But why do you call it a pre-excuse?"

"Because it gives them an excuse if they lose. After the match, they can say they lost because of their bad knee, or because they had a hangover, or whatever. They plant the excuse ahead of time, like taking out an insurance policy."

"I never thought about that before."

"Lots of players do it. They get in their pre-excuse before the match, so no matter what happens, their ego is happy."

"Why is that?"

"With their pre-excuse, their ego wins either way. If they lose, it isn't because they played badly or that you are a better player, it is because they had a bad knee or whatever. And if they win, that's like hitting the ego jackpot. They beat you even with a bad knee, which means they must be an incredible player. That's why the pre-excuse is one of the ego's favorite strategies."

"I guess a pre-excuse is better than a post-excuse."

"That's right. The pre-excuse is a much more refined ego protection system. If you throw out a post-excuse, you look like a poor loser, but with a pre-excuse, you are just being honest, sharing your pain and anguish with a fellow player. The less sophisticated ego player will use a post-excuse, but a sophisticated ego player will go for the pre-excuse."

"So you think Troy was lying, that he didn't have a bad knee."

"I'm not saying Troy was lying. Let's give him the benefit of the doubt and assume he had a bum knee. But that doesn't mean Troy should use a pre-excuse. He should have kept his knee problem to himself."

"But isn't it okay to use psychological warfare against your opponent?"

"Yes, there is a place for that, and we will get to that later. But this is another matter. It is bad sportsmanship. When you use a pre-excuse, you are just hedging your bets to protect your ego. It is not about using a psychological tactic during the game, it is about protecting, or propping up, your ego. The point is: If you want to be a good sport, don't make pre-excuses or post-excuses."

"Okay. I will watch that. I won't make pre-excuses or post-excuses. But what should I do if I lose? What if I had a bad knee or a headache?"

"Like I said, keep it to yourself. Simply congratulate your opponent, and tell them they played great. Leave it at that."

"Okay, I get it. So what else should I work on?"

"Keep watching what you do and say on and off the court. And watch what others do and say."

CHAPTER 10
A QUESTION ABOUT CALLS

For the next month, I kept my eyes and ears open. I had lots of opportunity because of a special indoor tournament at my club. It was special because it was the first time they'd ever had both men and women compete together in a singles tournament.

In the first round, I almost lost my first match to my friend Amy, who had won the women's championships a number of times. I had never played her before, and felt strange playing a woman. I felt it was mean to hit hard shots at her.

But Amy had no qualms herself. She hit cannonballs at me, barreling to the net, and putting away perfect volleys. Before I knew it, I was down 9 to 3 (the match was up to 10). At that point, I decided to forget that she was a woman, and play my normal game.

For some miraculous reason, I came back and won 10-9. Needless to say, I was very surprised by that outcome, and Amy was mad at herself but behaved like the great sport that she is.

During the following week, I won three other hard-fought matches, and found myself in the finals against Quinto, a former men's champion of the club.

The match got off to a good start. We both won our serves up to four all (Once again, we were playing first to 10.). Then things went off the rails. Quinto was serving well, but many of his serves were landing about six inches long of the service line. I kept calling them out, and I noticed that Quinto was getting annoyed. I figured he was annoyed with himself.

But then he served another one long, and I called it out. He walked to the net and glared at the service line. I could tell he was looking for the mark on the clay court. As is my habit in these situations, I walked up and drew a circle around the mark, which was clearly six inches out. He glared at me and then resumed serving.

I always get perturbed when someone questions my calls, but I don't let it bother me too much when it is an isolated incident. That's fine. All tennis players wonder if their opponents have called an out ball correctly. In the pros, they don't even trust the line judges. That's why they put in the electronic challenge system. So when two people are playing an important match, it's tough not to wonder about a call. That's why I didn't mind Quinto questioning my call. I figured he was just caught up in the match.

But then he did it again. After a long rally, he hit a ball wide, and I called it out. He came stomping to the net, and then actually walked over to my side of the court. Once again I had to circle the mark, which clearly showed that the ball was out.

Now I really felt that Quinto had crossed the line. In all my days playing tennis, only two or three people had ever come over my side of the court to check a line call. This was too much.

Quinto's behavior was really bothering me. I didn't know what to do. I felt very angry. By questioning my calls, was Quinto implying that I was cheating, that I was deliberating lying to win the match?

Then I felt guilty. Maybe I was wrong about those calls. Maybe I was unconsciously calling balls out. I also felt intimidated. I was afraid to call another one of his balls out, even ones that were out by 10 feet. All of these thoughts and feelings were swirling around in my head, and I still had to play the match.

Things just got worse. Quinto kept hitting serves out by a few inches, and I had to keep calling them out. Then on a game point, he hit a delicate drop shot over the net, and it landed just one ball length out. I was standing right over it, and practically vomited when I had to say "out."

Quinto was livid. "That was in," he argued.

"It was out," I said. "I'm sorry, but it was out."

"I saw it clearly," he said. "It was in."

I felt terrible. Had my eyes played tricks on me? Was I in some kind of delusion and so hell bent on winning that I was calling balls out when they were in? I didn't know what to do, so I said, "Okay, well, let's play it over."

Quinto was not very happy with the compromise. "That ball was in and I actually won the point, but fine, we can play the point over again, I guess."

I trudged back to the baseline, feeling absolutely horrible. I felt angry, hurt, guilty, indignant, shamed, embarrassed, and fed up with the whole match. I didn't care anymore. I didn't care about winning, because if I did, then Quinto would claim I had cheated to win. But if I gave up, then I was letting Quinto intimidate me. That might even be worse.

While all this was going through my head, Quinto served a ball three inches long, and I had to call it long. God. What a nightmare. Then on his second serve, I hit my return weakly into the net. Game Quinto. That put us in a tie-breaker.

I lost the tie-breaker 7 to 1. My heart wasn't in it. I didn't want to win anymore. I wanted to get off the court as soon as I could. I summoned up all my inner resources to congratulate Quinto on a "good" match, and did what Coach Conrad had told me to do; I said: "You played very well."

Then I went straight to the showers and drenched myself with cold water for 20 minutes until the steam stopped shooting out of the top of my head.

A few days later, I related the whole sorry Quinto saga to Coach Conrad. "I've never experienced anything like that in my whole life," I said. "I was completely unequipped to deal with someone questioning my calls in a match like that. It was crazy."

"That was a difficult situation," he commiserated. "No one likes it when someone questions their calls. Unfortunately, some people use it as a deliberate tactic to intimidate their opponent. Some people do it because they don't know any better. And some people get so caught up in winning that they lose sight of the fact they are being a bad sport."

"Do you think Quinto was being a bad sport?"

"Absolutely. His behavior was completely unacceptable. My rule is: Never, ever, question your opponent's calls. No matter what you think, even if you are 150 per cent sure your ball was in, never question your opponent's calls. Ever."

"You are really emphatic."

"I am. We have to remember that tennis is just a game. There are much more important things in life than winning a tennis match, even if it is the final at Wimbledon. When you question someone's calls, you are questioning their integrity. You are saying they are lying. My policy is: If someone questions my calls, then I don't play with them."

"But what if someone is deliberately calling my balls out? Should I not take them to task? Aren't they cheating?"

"No. You suck it up. As I said, you never question an opponent's calls, especially in a club match. If you think someone is doing that, you can just refrain from playing with them again. If you are playing in a serious tournament, if it comes to that, you can always ask someone to act as a referee and line judge if you want."

"It would have helped if we had some line judges in my match with Quinto."

"Yes. But it wasn't called for. It was a club match. Quinto should not have questioned your calls. Period. I mean, it is in his best interests. If he keeps doing it, no one will ever want to play with him."

"I don't want to play with him again, that's for sure. But I'm not sure what to do if someone else pulls the same stunt on me."

"There is one thing you can do if someone questions your calls. It takes a little nerve to do, but it will totally end the behavior."

"What's that?"

"When someone questions your calls, meet them at the net. Tell them you will give them every point they question."

"What do you mean?"

"Tell them that whenever they question your calls, you will simply give them the point."

"Why would I say that? They could then just question all my calls and they would win the match."

"But they won't do that."

"Why?"

"Because you have totally changed the game. You've turned the tables on them. You see, when they question your calls, they are implying you are cheating. That you are deliberately calling balls out so you can win.

"Well, now we have taken that out of the equation. In reality, when someone questions your calls, they are the one who is cheating. They are trying to intimidate you and get a point they didn't win. So now we shine the spotlight on that reality. Every time they question a call, they will win the point. If the ball was out, then they will win a point by cheating. It will be as plain as day."

"Why does that stop them, though? If someone is trying to cheat, they will still question your calls, won't they?"

"No, because their ego won't let them. When someone

questions a call, their ego convinces itself that it is their opponent who is cheating, even though they are the one who is cheating. Now, the ego doesn't have the benefit of that cover story. If they question a call and automatically win a point, they are the only one involved. The ego doesn't like that, because then it is clearer that it is actually cheating."

"I think I get it. If I tell them they can win a point simply by questioning my call, they won't do it, because they can no longer make it seem like I am cheating. How could I be cheating if I am willing to give away any point they want?"

"Exactly. It works every time."

Conrad was right. Since he gave me that tip, I've told three opponents that they can have the point if they question my calls. Never once did they question my calls again.

CHAPTER 11
YOU ARE NOT IN CONTROL

Having worked with Coach Conrad over several years, I was looking at tennis and my life in a whole new way. While I was still chasing a lot of toys, I was able to see that I was doing it. I noticed this when I started thinking I was a great tennis player, and when a few games later, I would think I was a terrible player.

I could see my ego playing with all of its toys: like checking out players on other courts and trying to decide if they were better or worse than me. I was also conscious of people watching me play, and of wanting to hit some spectacular shots to impress them. I could tell when I was getting greedy and wanting to win 6-0, instead of 6-4. I could see that when I was losing I would often adopt a "Who cares anyway?" attitude. I could also see that winning made me very happy, almost giddy, while losing made me very unhappy.

At first I was horrified by my thoughts and feelings. With my new perspective, I was casting a sharp light on the machinations of my mind, and it wasn't pretty. I felt really bad about myself, but Coach Conrad set me straight.

"You must remember, you are not your ego," he said. "Your ego is just something you have made up in your head. Think of it as an imaginary friend, or foe, if you prefer. So you don't have to take ownership of these thoughts and feelings."

"Does that mean I can do whatever I want? To act out on the impulses of my ego? That I am not responsible for my actions because my ego is imaginary?"

"Not at all. You are completely responsible for your actions. But thoughts and feelings are different from actions. You can have terrible thoughts, but if you don't act on them, you aren't hurting anyone except yourself.

"That's why it is so important to watch your thoughts. If you don't watch them, then you are more likely to take actions based on them, without pause for reflection. You will just keep reacting to everything that happens to you. So if you lose a point, you may have angry thoughts and throw your racquet. But if you are mindful that you are angry, and just watch the thoughts without taking ownership of them, you might not throw your racquet."

"So it's still okay to have angry thoughts, as long as I don't throw my racquet?"

"Everyone has angry thoughts sometimes. It is disappointing to lose a big point. It's annoying if someone cuts us off in traffic. But we don't have to act on those thoughts and feelings. If we become skillful at watching our thoughts, and not taking ownership of them, then we can make better choices. And then we might not throw our racquet or give someone the finger while driving."

"But I don't even want to have angry thoughts. Are you saying that I will still keep getting angry when I lose a point?"

"No one is perfect. You will still have angry thoughts, or mean thoughts, or jealous thoughts, but you will now be better equipped not to act on them in an inappropriate way. And over time, you will have fewer times when you feel angry, mean, jealous, or greedy, because you will no longer be clinging to the things that make you feel that way."

"What is the key thing we are clinging to in tennis that generates these negative thoughts?"

"Obviously, we are clinging to the idea that winning is good and losing is bad. We are clinging to the idea that if we lose, we are somehow diminished as a person, and if we win, we are somehow exalted as a person. If we can stop chasing those toys, then these negative emotions and thoughts will naturally dissipate."

"So I should stop trying to win?"

"Not at all. But remember your first insight, what got you started on this path. You learned that you could try to win and still be a good person. That was a good start because you realized that winning or losing had nothing to do with your worth as a person. Win or lose, you were still the same person."

"That has been very helpful."

"So yes, keep trying to win. It is important to give it your best shot, but try not to be attached to the outcome. This is important because you really have very little control over the outcome."

"But what if I try really hard, and practice, practice, practice? Won't that give me greater control over the outcome?"

"Do all of those things if you want. Train hard, and work hard.

Learn everything you can about tennis. But in the end, you will still have very little control of the outcome of a match because there are so many variables and conditions that you cannot control. If your opponent plays the best game of his life, you have no control over that. If a sudden gust of wind blows your ball out on match point, you have no control over that. If you sprain your ankle, there is likely nothing you can do about that either."

"You're right. There are so many factors that can cause you to lose. I guess that's why people make so many excuses. I used to always lose in the wind because I couldn't handle the way it affected my shots. It drove me nuts. I always blamed the wind when I lost in those conditions."

"It drove you nuts because your ego wanted to control everything, and you can't control the wind. But this principle also applies when you win. We like to think that we won because we practiced really hard, and we played great. Those could be contributing factors, but you may have also been exceedingly lucky, or your opponent could have felt sick, or his racquet broke, or the sun was in his eyes. The fact is, you have very little control over whether you win or lose."

"So what should I do, then?"

"Stop clinging to the idea of control. Don't try to control your shots, your game, or your life. It is a delusion, and stops you from expressing your true nature. It can also make you angry all the time."

"Why is that?"

"Our ego tries to control everything in order to achieve a certain ideal vision it has. If we are attached to this outcome, we get frustrated and angry when our expectations are not met. We cling to the idea of winning the match, and then we miss an easy shot or our opponent hits an incredible winner. If we want to control everything, we can get angry. So if you want to calm your mind, and decrease the frequency of negative thoughts, then you need to stop clinging to a desired outcome. Otherwise, you will never be truly happy."

"Why is that, again?"

"If we cling to the ideas of winning and losing, we will only be happy when we hit a good shot or win a match. Then when we miss a shot or lose a match, we will be unhappy. I mean, if you want happiness, that seems like a bad strategy."

"Okay, you are convincing me. I like the idea that I can still try to win. I do still want to win, but I will try to cling less to a desired outcome. But now I don't really understand the point of playing tennis if the ultimate goal isn't to win. What should I focus on instead?"

"Focus on keeping the game going. If you think about it, isn't that really the point? Playing games isn't about winning and then going home. It is about keeping the game going. It is about creating the conditions where everyone, whether they are winning or losing, feels good about playing more."

"How do I create those conditions?"

"There are lots of ways to do it. First, be generous. Congratulate your opponents on making great shots. Congratulate them when they beat you. Second, don't make excuses. As we talked about, don't make pre-excuses or post-excuses. Tell your opponent they played great and leave it at that. Third, have respect for your opponent, no matter what level they are playing at. Some people will be better than you, and some people won't be as a good as you. Regardless, treat them all with the same level of respect."

"That doesn't sound too hard."

"Well, it is harder than you might think. Because the ego is such a powerful player in our game, it doesn't want to do these things. It wants to beat the other guy, make excuses when it loses, and achieve permanent supremacy on the great ladder of life. So you have to watch your thoughts and your actions."

"Okay, I'll give it a try."

CHAPTER 12
RESPECT THE PRETZEL PUSHER

The following summer I made my annual switch to the tennis club near my house. It is a fantastic community club in an area of Toronto called "The Beach". The courts are right on the edge of Lake Ontario, which is nice because even on the hottest day of the summer, there is usually a cool breeze coming off the lake.

As usual, I signed up for the tennis ladder. I had been fortunate to win the ladder three years in a row, and was confident that I might do it again. Of course, I was trying not to be attached to this outcome, but I still had visions of extending my streak to four years running.

With these visions of grandeur in my head, I checked out the names of my opponents for the first month. I knew the other players in my box, except for one fellow named Ben. I wondered about him, and secretly hoped he wasn't that good. Good enough to give me a game, but not good enough to beat me. Watching that thought, I realized the extent of my attachments and clinging, and also felt bad about myself for thinking it.

Two weeks later, I had my first match with Ben. In the warm-up, my hopes soared because I quickly concluded that Ben was a B player at best, and maybe even a C player. He had the weirdest game I had ever seen. He played like a wound-up pretzel, twisting his body into strange contortions as he hit oddly sliced forehands and backhands. His serve was a seven-stage process; his racquet going every which way on the delivery.

He was also a pusher. He could run down practically every shot, but he didn't hit the ball very hard, and most of his balls landed around the service line. I foresaw a quick victory, even picturing myself writing 8-0 on the ladder board.

That's not exactly how it turned out. Ben won the toss, but elected to give me the serve. I chuckled at that one. *Only losers give up the serve when they win the toss*, I thought. Feeling full of gusto, I blasted my first serve at Ben, which spun to the right of his backhand. But Ben lunged for it, and hit a twisty, knuckle-ball type return that careened just over the net low to my forehand. Surprised, I ran up, reached down low with my racquet and hit my shot into the net.

Chalking that point up to pure luck, I offered up my next serve, this time to Ben's forehand. This resulted in an unexpectedly long rally. I pounded my ground strokes to Ben's forehand and backhand, and he kept pushing them back. At one point, I came to the net and he lobbed. I hit an overhead smash, but he got it and lobbed the ball again. On the third lob and smash, I pounded the ball right into the net.

Later on after the match, I realized that Ben's game had really gotten under my skin. He played like a back wall, getting everything back. When he won a point, I couldn't believe it. *He is such a terrible player*, I thought, *how could I lose even one point to him?*

Within short order, I was down 3-0, then 4-1, and then 5-2. At that point, my game had completely changed. I was pushing the ball back over the net like Ben. I was hitting forehand slices like Ben. And I was even starting to serve like Ben.

I was freaking out. I'm going to lose to Ben. What will the other players say? What will they think? Fear had taken over my being. This was a disaster. Sure enough, I lost 8-4.

I was infuriated with myself, but I remembered what Coach Conrad had instructed me to do. I told Ben he'd played great and congratulated him on his victory.

But it was all a facade. I didn't think Ben had played great. I thought he sucked, and that meant I sucked even more. Then I started making excuses to myself. *I lost because he has a weird game. I lost because he is a pusher. I lost because he slices his forehands, which wasn't right, and should not be allowed.*

Soon after, I confessed my sins to Coach Conrad, and he just laughed. "This is great. Ben will be one of your best teachers. It is good that you have Ben to play with."

"You mean, you want me to play Ben again?"

"I want you to play him a lot. He will really teach you about your ego and help you to stop clinging. But you need to do one thing: you need to respect Ben's game, and you need to respect Ben."

"What do you mean?"

"You lost to Ben because you didn't respect him and his game.

Just because he plays an odd game and hits weird shots, it doesn't mean he isn't a good player. But you didn't respect him. You thought you should wipe him off the court. And that made you fearful. When you lost the first few games, you became fearful that you would lose to a 'lesser' player. Your ego started thinking about what people would think if you lost to Ben. You thought about the shame and embarrassment that would befall you. So you started to play tentatively, and pushed the ball over the net, even mirroring his slice forehand. But if you had respected Ben as a player, and as a person, you would not have had the same problem."

"Why not?"

"If you respect Ben's game, then you won't worry if you lose. In actual fact, he beat you fair and square. During your match, he was the better player. There is no shame in that, just the shame that you have made up in your mind. So go back and play him more. Study his game. Figure out how to beat him, just like you would with any good player."

Over the summer, I played Ben 10 times. After another loss, this time much closer, I figured out that the best way to beat Ben was to work my way to the net by hitting most of my approach shots to his backhand. This set me up for a winning overhead or volley.

Using this strategy, I won the next nine matches, and had the confidence that I could beat Ben most of the time. I also came to respect Ben as a player. Although he had an unusual game, it worked for him. He had only started playing tennis four years earlier, and he practiced really hard at it. He was in top shape, and had a great attitude. He just loved to play, and he was a fantastic person to know.

I also enjoyed watching my fellow club mates grapple with the mystery of Ben. Up against Ben's slice and dice style, they were dumbfounded and enraged when they lost a game, and filled with shame when they were ultimately defeated. Sometimes, they were downright rude to Ben, screaming and berating themselves on the court, as if losing to Ben was the worst catastrophe to ever befall them.

From the sidelines, I could see how mean they were being to Ben. They weren't just mad that they missed a shot, they were doubly mad because they lost a point to Ben, whom they believed was the worst player in the world.

Of course, this all worked in Ben's favor. Because they didn't respect Ben and his game, they were gripped by fear, the fear of losing to Ben. And when this fear found its way into their bones, it crippled their game and soured their will. By not respecting Ben, they were doomed to lose, and they did.

In fact, Ben ended up second in the ladder that year. And I topped the ladder again by winning a final run-off against Ben. Because I respected his game, and worked hard to understand it, I prevailed handily in the final.

CHAPTER 13
A SEPARATE FICTION

With the coming of September, the outdoor conditions at the Beach club became more unpredictable. In one match against a player named Wayne, I had a really unpleasant experience. For one, Wayne had one of those cockamamie games like Ben. His balls twisted, sliced, and spun all over the place.

On top of that, the wind was swirling and howling. Wayne hit a shot over the net, and the wind blew it back over to his side of the court before I even had a chance to hit it. There was also a gaggle of kids on the next court getting a lesson. One ball after another kept rolling on the court. There were two or three lets in every game.

All of this chaos on the court drove me crazy. I was frustrated. Then angry. Then I was laughing. Then I raged at the wind. I was totally off balance. I wanted it all to stop, and looked forward to the peace and calm of playing in the bubble in winter. And although I beat Karl in a squeaker, I was completely stressed and miserable on my way home.

I told Coach Conrad about my windswept match, and he smiled in his typical guru fashion. "This is great. Another teaching moment for you."

"How so?"

"This is your chance to learn about the fiction of separateness."

"What does that mean?"

"Well, you were raging at all of those things because you wanted them to be different. You wanted Wayne to be different. You wanted the wind to be different. And you wanted the kids on the court beside you to be different."

"You're right. I did. But what has that got to do with separateness?"

"When you want things to be different, you feel separate from them. There is a 'you' that wants 'other things' to be different. This is the ego's desire for control—to control those things around it. This reinforces the idea that we are all separate, which is a fiction that the ego tries to convince us to believe."

"What do you mean? Aren't we all separate? I mean, I feel separate from you. I feel separate from a tree or a can of tennis balls."

"It seems that way on the surface. But we are not really separate; it is just an illusion. We are actually all one thing."

"Are you to telling me that we are all one?"

"That's a bit of a cliché, but it is close to the truth. In fact, we are all one with everything. There's the old joke about the Dalai Lama. He goes into a hamburger place and the server asks him what he wants, and he says that he 'wants one with everything.'

"That's a funny joke, but it is not really a joke. When we play tennis, we get this idea that we are separate. We are separate from the other player, we are separate from the ball, we are separate from the court. We think everything is a distinct thing. But in actuality, there is no real separation between you, the other player, the ball, and the court. It is all one single system, all interconnected, all linked together."

"Okay. I can't see that really, but I will go along with you."

"You don't have to take my word for it. Can you really say where 'you' begin and end? When you eat a sandwich, when does the sandwich stop being a sandwich and become you? Or look at it this way: could you exist without the world? If there was no world, where would you be? You see, you can't have one without the other. As I said, we are all part of one interconnected system. The idea of separateness is an idea, an illusion."

"But how will that help me with my tennis?"

"If you can truly understand this truth, it will help you with your tennis and your life. If you listen to your ego and believe that you are separate, you will suffer. You will suffer for three main reasons.

"One, you will use up a lot of energy in your mind keeping everything separate. It is like you are engaged in running a giant department store: sorting, categorizing, and labeling everything all the time. Using all of that psychic energy on this big labeling job doesn't leave a lot of energy for anything else. Then think about all of the energy you use in the material world trying to differentiate yourself and keep everything separate. That's a lot of energy expended.

"Second, trying to keep everything separate in our minds can make us aggressive because we are constantly defending our turf, proving we are better, stronger, faster, and smarter. That's why ultimately the ego is, at its core, angry and aggressive. It keeps trying to define itself, and because it knows that it does not actually exist, its core emotions are anger and aggression. It is angry because it knows it doesn't exist, and it is aggressive in trying to promote the fiction that it does exist. That's one of the reasons why we have so much violence and mayhem in the world."

"That's some really screwed-up stuff. But how does that affect my tennis game?"

"Well, let me tell you the third thing. Because we think we are separate from everything 'out there' we get irritated and annoyed by all of these things we consider to be unsatisfactory. You were annoyed by the wind, the kids on the court beside you, and Karl's crazy shots. These were unsatisfactory to you. You wanted the world to conform to your specifications and when they didn't, you suffered because you wanted them to be different. This was definitely a distraction. You couldn't focus properly on your tennis because you were focused on all of the things 'out there' that were bugging you. But if you could see that everything was part of one system, they wouldn't bother you so much."

"So what should I do about it? Feeling separate just seems natural."

"Well, if you are attached to the idea of separation on the tennis court, you won't be using your energy efficiently. Your brain, which uses most of your body's available energy, will work full tilt on its separation project. This means you will have less energy for performing well. Your mind will also be distracted and not engaged in the game itself. Finally, if your ego is in charge, then anger and aggression will dominate your emotions, and you will not perform well under those conditions."

"But don't anger and aggression help you beat the other guy? Don't these emotions actually give you energy?"

"It seems like they do. But the ego uses up so much energy so quickly that a more balanced player will outlast you, especially in a long match. As well, as we talked about months ago, aggressive players usually hit the ball too hard and make a lot of mistakes. They also get injured more."

"Why is that?"

"People who use their ego to play tennis get injured more because they are not listening to their body. Their ego is telling them to strive harder and go further. That sounds ambitious and laudable, but the ego often oversteps its bounds because it isn't the one that will perform the task. The body has to do that. So if the ego asks too much of the body, it will stretch beyond its limit, and then there will be an injury. That's why you want to continuously scan your body, both during a point and between points. Keep checking in and asking, 'What is my body telling me?'"

"I've never done that."

"Most people never do because in the western world, the intellect is considered more important. We are trained to listen to our mind, not our body. Some people are all in their head, and have no connection to their body. But our body is where all the real wisdom is. The mind speculates and makes theories about things, but the body actually knows what is going on. The mind can only live in the past or the future, which are fictions, but the body can only live in the present, in reality.

"So the more you are mindful of what is going on in your body, the more you will be in the present. And if you want to play tennis well, you have to be totally in the present. So be mindful of your body and you will play better tennis."

"That sounds like a contradiction: be mindful of your body."

"Yes, it does. But it is very important because if you are mindful of your body, then you will be less likely to get caught up in all kinds of thoughts about the past and the future. And then you will be less likely to have negative emotions in reaction to those thoughts. So you will be more balanced, and that will help you be a better tennis player."

"That all sounds excellent, but it flies in the face of everything I've ever learned. I've been taught that aggression on the tennis court and in the boardroom is a good thing. I've been taught to use my intellect to figure out strategies. That without at least some degree of aggression and intellect, I will fail."

"You have these core beliefs because of your *conditioning*."

"What does that mean, conditioning?"

"We are all a product of conditioning. These are all of the conditions that came together to make us who we are. These are the physical conditions of our body, but also the situation we were born into. It is also the cultural conditions that have been handed down for generations. All of these factors, plus many more, make us think, feel, and behave in a certain way.

"Part of the conditioning we have inherited is a tendency to be aggressive. This goes back thousands of years when humans were very vulnerable and had to fight against nature in order to survive. So we have been conditioned to believe that aggression is a sign of strength. It is hardwired into us, especially if we are male. But aggression is not a sign of strength. It is a sign of weakness, because when we are using anger and aggression as our emotional base, we are showing that we are actually not very strong."

"Why is that?"

"Well, at the heart of aggression is fear. If we are afraid of what we are facing, we often put on a mask of aggression to hide it. But we know in our hearts what is really going on. We know when we are aggressive that we are actually afraid, and then we know for certain that we are weak, not strong. This in turn makes us more aggressive, which makes us feel even more afraid and weak. It is a losing game."

"Wow, you're right. If you weren't afraid, you wouldn't need to be aggressive."

"You got it. So if you remember that all aggression is actually a sign of weakness, you are less likely to use it as a strategy and a way of being, and you will also understand it better in someone else. You will realize that your opponent, if they are being aggressive, is actually feeling afraid and weak."

"So on the tennis court, if I am being really aggressive, I will know that I am actually afraid. That's interesting. I will try that. But what is the alternative to being aggressive? What can I do instead?"

"You can practice equanimity. That means that no matter what happens, you remain calm and balanced. Think of yourself like a mountain in a raging storm. No matter how strong the wind, how loud the thunder, or how hard the rain, the mountain is unmoved. The storm is just an interesting and passing occurrence."

"I like that. I will try to be a mountain."

"Don't just try to be the mountain. Be the mountain. Be the mountain watching the storm. Just like the mother watching the child chasing the toys. You are the mountain watching the storm, which is both what is happening on the court, and what is happening in your mind. Watch the ball. Watch your thoughts. But no matter what happens, be the mountain."

"I love it. I'm going to try it."

"There is one other thing to keep in mind. As the mountain, you also realize that all phenomena is constantly arising and passing away. The storm comes and goes. The clouds come and go. The loud sound comes and goes. Nothing stays the same, nothing lasts. Everything is impermanent."

"How is that perspective helpful?"

"If you realize that all phenomena are impermanent, you will be less likely to cling to what happens, or try to push it away. You will just watch it come and go with equanimity. It will help you be a mountain."

"Anything else I should take away with me today?"

"Try to remember that you are not separate from what is happening around you. When something is bothering you, like loud kids playing on the court beside you, be mindful of what is happening. You will notice that it is not really the sound that is invading your space, it is actually you reaching out to grab that sound and turn it into something negative. The sound is just happening. It is just a wave moving through the air entering your ear drums. If it bothers you, it is because you turned it into something else, something you perceived as negative. But you are the one who did that, not the sound. And you did that because you think you are separate from the sound, and the kids who made the sound. That's why you suffer."

Leaving the club, I realized that Coach Conrad was really taking it up a notch. He was blowing my mind, but I was feeling energized and excited. The world was starting to look like a completely different place.

CHAPTER 14
FALLING OFF THE MOUNTAIN

For the next few months I tried to be a mountain on the court. No matter what happened, whether I won a point or lost a point, I maintained my equanimity. Negative thoughts would arise, and I would just let them go. Positive thoughts would also arise and I would let them go as well. I could see they were just thoughts. I didn't take ownership of them or get lost in them. They were simply mist passing by my mountain.

If I had a thought, I wouldn't follow it or add to it. I would break away from the thought by scanning my body between points. Doing this, I noticed that I hardly ever built up a big story. It was like I was cutting off the narrator of a story after the first couple of words. My internal narrator never got a chance to tell the whole story.

This made me more present. It gave me more energy and it made me a better player. I was winning more matches.

With my new mountain approach, I had great confidence about the upcoming summer tournament season. Maybe I would win a tournament. I had topped a lot of ladders and come in second several times in tournaments, but I had never triumphed. Now, as a mountain, maybe my time had come.

At the start of June, I signed up for the men's club tournament, which would run through the summer months and culminate in the finals at the end of September. I had a few close calls in the early rounds, but came out unscathed. I was playing strong consistent tennis, and when September came around, I found myself in the finals. I was laser focused and ready to close out the tournament. Nothing was going to stop me.

My opponent was a fellow named Graham. I had seen him hit with other people, but had never played him myself. He didn't look too tough. He had good style, yet he never came to net or hit the ball hard. Things were looking positive going into the final.

In the warm-up, I went through my routine, practicing ground strokes, volleys, overheads, and serves. I felt loose and energized. It was a warm day with just a breath of wind. Perfect conditions. As I had deduced earlier, Graham had a pretty solid game, but he didn't hit the ball hard. He also had a relatively weak backhand. I was ready.

Graham won the toss and elected to serve. On the first point, he hit an easy serve to my backhand, and I returned it crosscourt to his forehand. He returned my ball with a slow high arch to my backhand. Then I aimed a slice down the line, but I misjudged and the ball went wide. 15-love Graham.

And so it went. I kept trying to hit hard balls, and Graham just lobbed them back. I would come to the net, and he would lob over my head. Losing the first set 6-2, I had completely forgotten about being a mountain. I wasn't even a mole hill.

I can't believe I'm losing to this guy, I thought. *I'm a better player than him, I should be winning. I can't lose another tournament in the finals, I just can't.*

All of these thoughts and words turned into a big story: *I am a choker. I can't win a tournament. Who am I kidding?*

In the second set, I started playing like Graham. Instead of my usual hard shots, I moon balled most of my groundstrokes. The pace of the rallies slowed down. I was pushing my shots, afraid to make a mistake. I had also given up on coming to the net, scared that he would lob over me again. Some of the rallies lasted 50 shots or more.

I was also feeling completely stressed out. I could feel a deep gloom descend over me as I concluded that glory was not waiting for me at the end of the match.

Sure enough, Graham won the second set 6-3, and before I knew it, the whole thing was over. I was so disappointed. I put on my best face and gave Graham a hearty congratulations, but inside I was sinking. I'd blown my last chance to win a tournament, and I could have beaten him. At 51 years of age, I figured it would be unlikely I'd ever again get to the finals of another tournament, let alone win one.

I was also discouraged because my much ballyhooed inner mountain had collapsed just when I needed it. All of the psychological training I had done with Coach Conrad had been a complete waste of time. What was the point of all this ego busting, if it didn't help me win a tournament?

I dreaded meeting up with Coach Conrad for our next lesson. I was embarrassed to tell him I had lost—let's face it, choked—and ashamed I had failed the mountain test. As customary, though, he came back with a surprising take on the whole thing.

"It's a good thing you didn't win that tournament," he said.

"Why is that?"

"First, let's give you credit for reaching the finals. Most of the players in the tournament were in their 20s and 30s. For a 51-year-old guy, that is an achievement in itself. Remember, 10 years ago your tennis game had deteriorated, and you were in terrible physical shape. Now look at you. You are playing the best tennis of your life, and you are in great shape. You've also learned a lot about yourself, and about tennis. Would you have ever dreamed that you would be in the finals of a tennis tournament at age 51? These are all good things to be grateful for."

"You're right. I am grateful, but I still think I should have won the tournament."

"As I said, it's a good thing you didn't win the tournament. You are still too attached to the outcome. You are still clinging to stories. You believe you have to win a tournament to feel good about yourself. As well, you have this other story that you don't deserve to win a tournament. Somewhere deep down, you don't think you are worthy of winning a tournament, or winning anything, for that matter. I still think you believe you are a bad person if you beat someone."

Coach Conrad's words made me wince. He was butchering me. But he spoke the truth.

"I hate to admit it, but it's true," I conceded. "I really wanted to win that tournament. I wanted to win it so bad, to prove to myself that I was a winner, not a loser. I guess I feel like a loser in my heart of hearts, and now I have the proof."

"But you're not a loser. No one is a loser. That's just vertical relating. It's just a story you are telling yourself about yourself. It is not reality."

"I feel really bad because I fell off the mountain. In the other matches in the tournament I was Mount Everest, but in the final I wasn't even an ant hill."

"Sure, it's disappointing that you lost in the final, but if you had won, you might not have learned a lesson. You would have simply bolstered your ego, and glossed over your deeper feelings. But if you can really learn from what happened, you have an opportunity to grow as a person, which you might not have done if you had won."

"I'm willing to put a silver lining on it. I might as well."

"If you can use this experience as a foundation for learning about yourself, it will be worth it. Unfortunately, that's not what most people do. When they lose, they just make excuses or put it out of their mind. In your case, there's so much you can do with this experience as long as you admit that something much deeper was going on out on the court."

"There was definitely something deeper going on. That's for sure. On paper I should have beaten him. But my thoughts and feelings got in the way."

"There are a number of things you can take away from the

match. You were obviously very attached to winning the tournament. The stakes were extremely high for you. You saw it as your last chance to win a tournament before you pick out your walker and move to a nursing home. This increased your level of striving."

"Is striving bad? I thought striving was a good thing."

"There is nothing wrong with working towards achieving goals. If you are attached to the outcome, however, you will put too much striving energy into it. Striving energy is fueled by the ego. It pushes you forward, but it can push you in the wrong direction."

"Why is that?"

"Because the ego has the wrong intentions."

"What kind of intentions?"

"The ego's intention is to seek fame and glory, to rise higher on the totem pole. Its goal is to prove it's better than others."

"I know. The more I become aware of my ego, the more I realize that's what it's up to."

"That's why this is a good lesson. You weren't ready to win the tournament because you were driven by your ego with the wrong intentions."

"You're right. I was focused too much on winning the tournament, and when I started to lose in the match, I was gripped by fear."

"How did your body feel?"

"It felt tense and wound up. I pushed harder and harder, but it didn't work. Graham just kept hitting the ball back, without any pace. It was so frustrating."

"It definitely sounds like striving energy. The key is to understand that this kind of energy, striving energy, is not very effective. It uses up much more energy than is required for the task. It is also unnatural, so if you are playing a physical sport like tennis, it makes your game unnatural. You can see it when players start off by hitting the ball really hard, and then switch to a push game in the middle of a match. When they are hitting the ball hard, the ego is striving to crush the other player, and when they are pushing the ball, the ego is afraid to make a mistake. Either way, they are not playing naturally, and in a close match, striving energy will probably result in a loss."

"That's exactly what happened. I came out all full of piss and vinegar, and quickly devolved into a sniveling mass of fear. It was horrible."

"I've learned that playing a club level match is a lot different from what happens in the pros. Generally speaking, in the pros, it is the player who wants it most who will win the match. But at the club level, it is usually the player who wants it the least who will win."

"Hey, what a minute. That's the opposite of everything I've ever heard. You mean if I don't care about winning, I will win more matches?"

"You got it. You lost your match because you wanted it more than Graham did. It sounds like Graham didn't care if he won or lost. That's why he was so relaxed. I don't mean that he didn't try to win, or didn't enjoy winning, it just wasn't the life and death struggle for him that it was for you. He wasn't using striving energy. He was using his natural energy. And I wager that's one of the main reasons he won."

As always, Coach Conrad's observations were counterintuitive to me. "You mean I should try less hard when I am playing."

"Not really. You could experiment with that, but it would only scratch the surface. You need to dig deeper and discover what's going on deep down inside of you. That's why it is such a good opportunity. You can use tennis to learn more about yourself; you can become more aware of your conditioning and your unconscious core beliefs. That's the true benefit of playing a game like tennis. Sure, it is great exercise and fun to play, but it is also a chance to learn more about yourself."

"Okay. So what do I do now?"

"When you are playing tennis, be aware of your striving energy. Be aware of who is actually playing. Is it your ego striving to win the point and win the match? Or is it your natural self in flow with the game?"

"How will I know that?"

"Just be aware of what is going on. Watch your thoughts. What are you thinking on the court? What are you feeling? Are you lost in a big story? If so, what is that story? Ask yourself if you feel disconnected or connected. Does it feel like there is a 'you' playing out there, or is there no real distinction between you, the ball and court, and the other player? Are there a bunch of parts, or is there one unified system?"

"That sounds like a tall order, but I will try it."

"Another thing to bear in mind is the distinction between confidence and intention. Most of us are focused on keeping up our confidence. We use little mantras to boost our spirits. We tell ourselves that we are a good player, maybe even a great player. We pump our fists when we win a big point. But all of this confidence building is actually counter-productive."

"Why is that?"

"When you work hard to boost your confidence, you are actually telling yourself you have no confidence. Otherwise, why would you have to work so hard to bolster it? If you truly have deep confidence, you don't have to bolster it. It is bedrock. But when you are working hard to prop yourself up, it is obvious that you actually think you have no confidence. So it is a vicious circle."

"So what should I focus on?"

"Focus on intention. What are your intentions in playing tennis? What are your intentions in your life, in your business, and in your relationships? What are you really trying to do?"

"I've never thought about that before."

"Most people haven't because if they do they might realize their intentions are less than ideal. And if they admit that honest truth, then they might have to make some big changes in their life. That's pretty scary."

"I can see that. In fact, I don't think I've ever thought about my intentions. I don't use that word in my vocabulary, unless I'm talking about someone else."

"It's a lot easier to point out someone else's intentions than to examine our own," Conrad said. "But that's just the first step. By examining your true intentions, you have the chance to change them so they better reflect your values."

"You mean our intentions can be counter to our values? I thought they would be aligned naturally."

"In the deepest sense they are. But on a superficial level, when the ego is in control, they are often misaligned. You see, the ego's intentions are often not very commendable. The ego's intentions are to seek domination, status, power, control, and material wealth. So if we get caught up in what the ego wants, then those will be the intentions that are driving our actions."

"That's not good."

"No. But the good news is that the ego is not us, and it doesn't actually exist. So these ego-driven intentions are not hard to deal with, as long as we see them for what they are. And that starts with being honest with ourselves: asking ourselves what are the intentions that are driving us? Are they our ego's intentions, or our deeper, more true intentions?"

"Are you saying we have two levels of intentions: our ego intentions and then our deeper, true intentions?"

"That's right. If we look closely, we realize that we have deeper intentions that truly reflect our values. But they are usually hard to see because they are masked by our ego's intentions, which are also hard to see because we are usually denying them."

"That's incredible. I've really never thought about things this way before."

"Once you see your intentions for what they are, it's not hard to see what is going on."

"But what about criminals and terrorists? Do they have better intentions deep down?"

"That's one of life's great debates, and we won't solve it here. It's my belief that when people commit criminal acts, it's because their ego intentions have taken complete hold of them, and they are not awake to what could be better intentions deep down."

"Don't they say that the road to hell is paved with good intentions?"

"That expresses exactly what I am trying to say. If we cover our ego's intentions with a façade of good intentions, we can cause all kinds of destruction. So we have to get a handle on this, or we will all suffer."

"So what should I do when playing tennis?"

"Do some soul searching. Ask yourself two questions. 'What are my ego's intentions?' Then, 'What are my deeper, true intentions that more closely correspond to my values?' It is helpful to write down the answers, and look at what you wrote from time to time."

"Then what?"

"Then when you are playing tennis, check in and see which type of intentions are at play. Is it your ego intentions, or your deeper, truer intentions? You will learn a lot about yourself, and you might notice that you are having a different experience out on the court."

"Okay, I'll give it a try."

CHAPTER 15
LEARNING THE MACHINE LANGUAGE

When I was a junior tennis player, I dreamed of being ranked in the top 10 in my region. Starting at age 11, I competed in junior tournaments, and became friends with many of the best tennis players my age. Although I did pretty well, I never achieved a top 10 ranking in my age group. Some of my friends were ranked in the top 10, and I felt envious of their status.

This envy built up inside of me as a powerful unmet need that never went away. So at age 51, I decided to take one more stab at getting a top 10 ranking, this time in the over-45 senior level. I figured it was my last chance at fame, if not fortune.

In my first match at a province-wide open tournament, I felt very nervous heading out onto the court. I was used to playing at my club, but this was a completely different level of competition. The whole experience felt uncomfortable. It was all very official, and everyone took things quite seriously.

Before the match, an official read out a detailed list of rules to us, stressing that abusive and rude conduct was not permitted. The fact that the official needed to read these rules to two grown men over 45 made me wonder what I had gotten myself into. Was this tennis, or a geriatric version of world federation kick boxing?

The look of Igor, my opponent, didn't put me at ease. He was a stocky, stout guy built like a refrigerator. He had the mien of a surly gang member. He never cracked a smile, and when we changed ends, he never looked at me. When I tried to engage him in some idle chit-chat, he looked annoyed, and kind of grunted. He was all business.

Igor had one major strength as a tennis player: his serve. They were cannonballs, both the first and second. Bearing down on me, these projectiles seemed literally life threatening. I didn't want to catch one in the wrong place.

Although Igor missed a lot of serves, and double faulted occasionally, when his serves did go in, they were virtually impossible to return. I barely got my racquet on them. Throughout the match I only got back about 10 of his serves. On the return of serve, I felt rattled.

On my serve, things were better. Beyond his serve, Igor wasn't much of a player. He looked like one of those monstrous mountain trolls from The Lord of The Rings. He had a hard time navigating his refrigerator bulk around the court, and his ground strokes were feeble and inconsistent.

So I decided to move him around the court as much as possible with drop shots, lobs, and wide ground strokes. This approach worked great, and I won most of my service games. But he managed to break me once in each set, so I walked off the court having lost 6-4, 6-4. My final memory of the match was having my hand crushed by Igor's gargantuan paw when I congratulated him on his victory.

During that winter I played five other senior tournaments. I lost in the first round of every tournament, sometimes in biblical proportions. I lost 6-0, 6-0 to the top player in Canada, barely winning a point. That was humbling. A few times I won a match in the consolation round, which gave me a little reassurance that I wasn't necessarily the worst player in the tournament.

At the end of the season, I was ranked 34th out of 40 players (I got a few points for winning consolation matches). Not exactly the stellar success I had been hoping for.

I felt discouraged, and resigned myself to the notion that I would never be ranked in the top 10. In the darkest recesses of my mind, I pined that I would never be in the top 10 of anything. The question was: Should I continue with these senior tournaments in the next season, or give up the quest altogether?

I brought my soul-searching to Conrad, who was characteristically philosophical about the whole matter.

"This is exactly what I was talking about when I told you to focus on your intentions," he said.

"I did that," I returned defensively.

"Your primary intention was to reach the top 10. Is that right?"

"That's why I signed up for the tournaments," I told him, feeling slightly shamed.

"So when you ended up ranked 34th, how did that make you feel?"

"Terrible. I figured I completely failed. Now I'm wondering if I should keep going, or just give up the quest altogether!"

"What makes you think you failed?" Conrad asked me sharply.

"I'm just not good enough for that level. Those guys are incredibly good. They are way more talented than I am. I'm out of my league."

"No, that's not it. You lost because you had the wrong intention. Your intention to get into the top 10 was the reason you didn't make it to the top 10."

"I disagree," I said. "I lost because those guys are just better than me. That's it. But at least I'm honest about it."

"Yes, it's not very likely that you can beat the number one player in Canada. No matter what you do, you might never be able to beat him. But there were other players you could have beaten but didn't because you had the wrong intention."

"Okay, you've been so helpful every other time, I'm willing to listen," I said, settling in for the lesson to come.

"When you made it your intention to get into the top 10, you let your ego take over the whole enterprise. Everything that happened in the matches, even before and after, was centered on the goal of getting into the top 10. You were ensnared in the trap of vertical relating. This affected your moods, your actions, and your performance. Igor intimidated you because you had set the stakes so high. Instead of being just another player, he was, in your eyes, a gatekeeper who stood in your way of top 10 nirvana. Seen in this context, Igor got bigger and bigger. He was no longer just another player, he became an idea."

"What do you mean by that—an idea?"

"When we are caught up in ego, we perceive reality though a

veil of ideas. Nothing is just what it is. A cigar is not just a cigar. There is an idea attached to everything. In this case, Igor wasn't just Igor, he was someone who was standing in your way to the top 10. And once that idea took hold, it became your reality. And without being aware of it, you then proceeded to make it the truth by letting him win."

"I didn't let him win, he beat me fair and square."

"Maybe, but it is more likely that it was your idea of him that defeated you, not the man himself."

"Did I start telling myself a story about Igor?"

"Perhaps. You have become quite skilled at noticing when a story takes hold. But ideas are even more insidious. Ideas are not always expressed with words. They are often constructed with feelings and emotions, and not articulated with words, either verbally or mentally."

"So I built my idea of Igor around my feelings, not words."

"That's right. That's why you felt so nervous. In this case, your idea of Igor was built of feelings, not words."

"Wow, that sounds bad."

"It's not bad. It is just the next step in your quest to discover who you really are. Now you need to be mindful of your feelings, and investigate what is actually going on. And also investigate the overall intention that might be causing those feelings."

"That sounds hard."

"It isn't really. All of your feelings are expressed in your body. When you engage in tennis, even before you go out on the court, check in with your body. Are you feeling nervous, or excited, or pumped up? Are you feeling inadequate or dominant? When you give it a try, you will discover that watching your feelings is much more powerful than simply noticing your stories."

"Why is that?"

"It is easy to get caught up in a story, and project its origin onto the outside world. It is easy to notice your stories because you can make them all about other people and things, not about yourself. As well, being mindful of your stories, while useful, can be kind of intellectual. You can be spot-on about the crazy story you are telling yourself, without being aware or honest about the underlying feelings that are generating that story. So you are only part way to the true insight you might need to have about yourself."

"That makes sense," I said.

"But your feelings are much more personal. Only you experience them. Even if you try to explain them to other people, words are often inadequate. If you are mindful of your feelings, then you are getting to the core of what is really going on. If you feel scared or sad or alone, these are very important feelings because you can now investigate what is really behind them. You are much closer to getting to the heart of the matter."

"I wonder what feelings I was really feeling."

"Well, you tell me, they are your feelings."

"I guess I was feeling nervous and kind of scared."

"Why do you think you were feeling nervous and scared?"

"I was definitely intimidated. I didn't want to make a fool of myself. Actually, I felt like a bit of a fraud. I didn't want them to discover that I wasn't really that good a player."

"Did you think Igor was a great player?

"I don't know. He seemed really big and imposing, and frightening."

"What if Igor was a member of your club? How would you feel when playing him in that setting?"

"It would have been different, I'm sure. He would have been just another club player. But at the regional level, Igor seemed bigger and tougher."

"That's because you had two major ideas going on. One was the idea that you didn't belong in the big leagues. Two, that Igor was an obstacle in getting to the top 10."

"Yup, you've got that right. And that's why I was so nervous and scared. The two ideas made me feel that way. So I guess, if I didn't have those ideas, things would have gone better out there."

"You also had another idea going on."

"What was that?"

"You had the idea that you couldn't return Igor's serve."

"That's for sure. After the first few games, I was convinced his serve was too hard."

"And how did that make you feel?"

"Scared and intimidated."

"So there you go. The idea created the feeling, and it was that feeling that defeated you, not Igor's serve itself."

"Holy mackerel! You're right. It was my feelings based on an idea that beat me. Once I was convinced that Igor's serve was unbeatable, that was it. I didn't even really try to hit it back. Game, set, match."

"Now you're getting it."

"But here's a question. What causes these ideas? And how can I get better ideas?"

"The solution is not to replace one idea with another. That is just a fool's game. You could try to change the idea to 'I can hit back Igor's serve.' But that's not going to work, because you are still playing tennis with ideas. And the first time you miss one of Igor's serves, you will start questioning your new idea, and fall back to the old idea. Then you will go from feeling competent and powerful, to feeling inadequate and weak."

"So what do I do instead?"

"Focus on your intentions."

"Why is that?"

"Because it is intentions that create ideas and the feelings. It is where it all starts. It is kind of the machine language of your tennis game."

"What's machine language?"

"That's the deep code that is written right into the core central processor of a computer. We are familiar with software like Word or Power Point, and operating systems like Windows or Apple OS, but few of us have ever heard about machine language. And that's the parallel I want to draw here. Your thoughts are like a software program. Your feelings are like an operating system. And your intentions are like a machine language. They are the deep core processor that controls your feelings and your thoughts."

"You're saying that my intentions control my feelings and my thoughts?"

"Sort of. Control is probably not the right word. Let's put it this way: Your intentions set up the conditions for what thoughts and feelings you will have."

"How so?"

"If your primary intention is to get to the top—in your case to the top 10—then you will see the world through that lens. Everything will be judged either good or bad, depending on whether it helps you achieve that goal. You perceived Igor as a threat to that goal, so you had certain feelings about him, such as fear, which made you think certain thoughts, such as, 'I'm not good enough to return his serve.'"

"So my intention to get to the top 10 actually made me fear Igor's serve, and then I thought that I couldn't return it. And because I had this idea, it became a self-fulfilling prophecy."

"That's right. Your intention to get into the top 10 produced ideas in your mind that actually undermined your ability to get there."

"I think I get that. So I guess the answer is to change my intentions, is that it?"

"Maybe. The important thing is to be aware about your intentions, and be honest about them. Then you can choose what intentions you want to focus on. But that is the hard part for most people."

"Why is that?"

"It's hard because intentions are rarely discussed in our culture. The word is not common in our collective vocabulary. As a result, many people are not able to articulate their intentions, or to judge their true intentions honestly. Just like a machine language, our intentions are often buried so deep in our psyche that we don't even know they are there."

"I think I'm in that category. I've never really thought about my intentions, certainly not when it comes to tennis. I never really questioned them. I assumed that the intention was to beat the other guy, win tournaments, and get to the top."

"But now you have the chance to look closely at your intentions, and decide if they are actually working for you."

"Right. So you're saying that my intention to get into the top 10 may actually have undermined my ability to get there."

"That's right. If your ego sets the intention, then you are bound to get into trouble. If your ego is running the show and setting the agenda, you are going to feel, think, and do things that might work against your long-term interests. When your goal is thwarted, you will get frustrated and angry. If you are winning, you will feel elated and powerful. This will set up alternating thoughts of inadequacy and grandiosity. You will also alternate between thoughts about the past and thoughts about the future.

"Either way, you won't play in the moment. You will become

distracted and not play your best. You will also play through a barrier of ideas and stories. All of which will have a negative effect on your tennis game. The weight of the ideas and stories is like shackles tied to your legs. They don't help you feel free, light, and loose."

"So what should my intentions be?"

"That is not something I can answer for you. You can't get your intentions from someone else. They aren't something you can download from the Internet. You have to think and feel deeply about your intentions, and decide for yourself what you really want them to be."

"Can't you even give me a little suggestion?"

"My suggestion is that you keep playing. Keep watching your thoughts and your feelings. Investigate where they are coming from. Look for the intentions at the core of your feelings and thoughts. Watch your ego at work. And focus on the good."

"What do you mean by that?"

"Focus on what is good about playing tennis, no matter what's happening in the game or the score. When you miss a shot or lose a game, steer your mind towards what is good about the experience at that moment."

"So you want me to practice positive thinking."

"No, that is a superficial way of looking at it. Focus on the things about your experience that are not conditional on winning or losing."

"Like what?"

"You'll have to determine that for yourself. But here's a couple of examples. You can focus on how it feels to share your experience with your opponent. What does it feel like to be connected to another person in this way? Or focus on what effect gravity has on the game. Be grateful for gravity."

"You want me to be grateful for gravity?"

"Sure. Imagine tennis without gravity."

"That's true. You couldn't play tennis in outer space. Without gravity there would be no tennis."

"And you can be grateful for the 'good' of gravity at any time. It doesn't matter what's happening in the match itself."

"Just when I'm playing tennis?"

"You can do it any time, but tennis is a great place to start. Think of the game as a laboratory for self-exploration. Watch how you respond to the ups and downs of a match. Tennis, like all games, is a safe place to learn about ourselves. You can then take that new self-knowledge out into the rest of your life."

"Okay. I'll do that. I'm going to sign up for the men's tournament again. You know the one where I lost in the finals last year."

"Good luck."

CHAPTER 16
CULTURAL SUGGESTIONS

As I told you, dear reader, I had never won a tournament. I had won some ladders, and had come second a dozen times, but I had never won the big prize. Conrad was right about a lot of things, and he was especially right about one thing: Because I wanted to win so badly, I made tennis a life or death struggle in my mind. The notion that I would come in second again made me hesitate to even sign up for the men's tournament. I also contemplated the idea that it would be better to lose in the first round than to lose again in the finals.

The fact that I hadn't closed the deal and won a tournament made me question my worth as a human being. It seemed like there was something wrong with me. Maybe I was afraid of success or actually achieving my goals. Thinking about it was driving me crazy.

Then it hit me. Maybe thinking about it was the crazy thing. Maybe I should stop thinking about tennis and start experiencing it instead. To me that was a startling insight. Tennis had always been a thinking game to me. That's what I loved about it. It wasn't just a physical activity, it was a thinking game. I loved thinking about new strategies, and analyzing the psychology behind the game. But now I wondered if I had taken it too far.

So I decided to sign up for the tournament, and instead of

thinking, I would start experiencing.

My first three matches of the tournament were a breeze. I beat the first guy 10-1 (we played up to 10, not the normal six game sets.) He had a complete meltdown on the court, and accused me of cheating on a number of my calls. I told him, as was now my habit, that he could have any point he wanted. All he had to do was question one of my calls.

To my surprise, he actually took me up on it a couple of times. But it didn't matter. He wasn't going to win the game, let alone the match. I was astonished that someone could be so caught up in a match that he would behave in such a manner. After all, he was completely outmatched. He was actually a great squash player and would have creamed me on the squash court, so it didn't make any sense for him to go so crazy playing tennis against me. But he did.

I especially enjoyed the moment when he flung his racquet against the back fence and screamed a few choice obscenities. I chuckled to myself, but then noticed that a youngster on the adjacent court was watching his antics with great interest. That gave me pause—what kind of example was my opponent setting for the next generation?

Moving on from there, my second-round opponent was a much more skilled player. He was about a foot taller than me, and hit every ball like a blast from a shot gun, with lots of power but little accuracy. I drove him crazy by bringing him to the net on drop shots, and then lobbing over his head. With his prodigious mass, he couldn't stop the forward momentum on his approach to the net, and was therefore unable to reverse direction and run back to retrieve the lobs.

After three games of this, he was beside himself. I could see that he thought I was a pusher, but I didn't care. I was already up 3-0, having broken his serve twice. A few times my lob wasn't high enough and he was able to hit a smash. But they were no ordinary smashes. They were the smashes of Thor. He pounded the smashes so hard that a few of them bounced over the back screen and into the parking lot beyond. *A little bit of overkill*, I thought.

The interesting thing was that he thought I would be intimidated by his power. Actually, I saw it as his weakness. I could tell he was so frustrated by what was going on that he took it out on the poor ball. I knew that the harder he hit his smashes, the more frustrated and scared he was.

In this way, his power smashes actually gave me confidence. I walked away with a 10-2 victory. Last I heard, he quit the club, and hasn't played tennis since. Too bad.

My third opponent was the toughest in the early rounds. He was a classic baseliner. He chased down every ball, and got everything back. He wasn't a pusher by any means, but he didn't put a lot of oomph into his ground strokes. I could tell he was nervous, and he never came to the net.

While I was not comfortable at the net myself, I decided to go for it and build each point towards a volley or a smash. I also noticed that he preferred to run around his backhand, so I started the point by hitting wide to his forehand, and then came to the net on a wide shot to his backhand. Forced to hit his passing shot on his weak side, he was undone. But I also had to make sure I finished the point with a solidly hit volley. Otherwise, he would run it down, and put the ball away. This match forced me to play outside my comfort zone, and that's why I was so pleased to come away with a 10-7 win.

But I was more pleased about something else. While I had done a lot of thinking about my opponents, and used different strategies, I had also focused on experiencing tennis more than just thinking about it. At the end of each point I checked in with my body. How was my body feeling? Sometimes I could sense tension in my gut, or a pain in my knee. I practiced dwelling on these sensations, rather than ignoring them or wishing they would go away. I just felt them.

I also focused on the "good" of the experience. Here I was doing what I loved, playing tennis. What could be better than that? I savored the blue sky and the wisp of a cooling breeze. I luxuriated in the green of the clay courts, and felt the softness of the ball in my palm. I absorbed a deep feeling of connection with the other players on the courts, all of us engaged in this wholesome, life-affirming activity.

I kept all of these feelings to myself. Although I knew this new approach was making my tennis more enjoyable and dramatically improving my performance, there was no way I was gong to share my experience with others. It all seemed a bit strange to me, so I kept it all to myself.

I even focused on the good of gravity. When playing a point, I felt in my body the interesting impact of gravity. How gravity was keeping me anchored to the court. How gravity created the rainbow curve of the tennis ball as we hit it from one side of the court to the other. I realized that without gravity there would be no tennis. So I actually felt grateful for gravity. But I definitely didn't tell anyone about my new-found appreciation for gravity.

And that was just the beginning. By taking in these new elements of the tennis experience—beauty, connection, and gratitude—I noticed I became less attached to the egocentric elements of the game: vertical relating, competitive aggression, and unmet emotional expectations.

I could see clearly when I slipped up and fell back into these less skillful modes of playing tennis. Which I did. There were plenty of times when I berated myself for missing a shot, or fell into a reverie about winning the tournament. But these thoughts and feelings were now counterbalanced by another way of experiencing tennis at a more profound, wholesome level.

In the semi-finals of the tournament, I was up against an old nemesis. He was about 15 years older than me. We had been playing matches against each other for more than 35 years, ever since I was a teenager. In all those years, I had never beaten him. Our matches were always close, sometimes coming down to a tie-breaker, but I had never won. I knew I had a psychological problem playing him.

After all those years, I had become convinced that I would

never beat him. This time, though, I was determined to break through and beat him. So I did something radical. I booked a court to play someone else for an hour before my real match. I was taking a risk because I might exhaust myself. But I banked on the idea that the hour warm-up would give me a huge advantage.

And that's what happened. In the warm-up game, I kept my mind on totally enjoying the experience. I hit every ball without fear, and felt grateful for even being on the court. By the end of the hour my strokes were smooth and consistent. My muscles were warmed up, and I felt great.

Then my long-time opponent showed up. I didn't tell him about my 60-minute warm-up, but he could see I was sweating and all warmed up. I went into the locker room and put on a fresh set of tennis clothes, and then re-emerged onto the courts.

Within 40 minutes, I took out my opponent 10-0. He was stunned. So was I. But most important, I realized my warm-up game wasn't only about warming up my body, it was also about warming up my attitude. When I got into the match, I also warmed up by trying see the good in everything. I wasn't worried about the score or if I would lose again to him. I was just having a great time, and it translated into a big win.

To his everlasting credit, my opponent congratulated me profusely, not just for winning the match, but also for breaking his streak after 35 years. As he said good-naturedly: "It's about time you beat me."

Up next was the final. I'd never felt more ready to win a

tournament. *This is going to be my year*, I told myself. But alas, it was not meant to be. When the day came for the finals, the storm clouds moved in and we were rained out for three days. That gave me too much time to think. Doubt crept in. I felt nervous. Then we had to play the match at night under windy conditions.

My opponent arrived at the court with a bandage on his knee, complaining about a torn muscle. *Oh no*, I thought: *pre-excuse!* I had also never played him before. He had one of those quirky games with lots of strange shots. Pretzel-pusher! His balls skidded and twisted like I had never seen before.

It was the perfect storm. It was just too much. I fell back into my old ways. I got scared and starting pushing my balls. I ran away in my mind, chasing a story about my inadequacy. He jumped ahead quickly and won the first set 6-3.

Then I felt dejected. I got a sick feeling in my gut. *Here we go again,* I thought. *Another loss in the finals.* I felt shamed and embarrassed. I didn't feel grateful at all. And then I felt annoyed. *Come on. There's nothing wrong with his knee,* I thought. *He's a pusher. That's not fair. How did this guy get into the finals anyway? The other side of the draw must have been a joke. He shouldn't even be playing in this level. Who let him in?*

I also railed against the wind. *I hate playing outside. This wind is driving me crazy.* I went over the edge and abandoned everything I had ever learned from Coach Conrad. An epic fail. I lost the second set 6-2, and found myself once again offering my congratulations to an opponent in the finals. At the awards banquet, he got a big trophy, and I got a chorus of better luck next time.

It was two months before I had recovered enough to book a lesson with Conrad. He just smiled when I told him my sorry tale.

"That's really too bad," Conrad said. "But that's the way it goes. Obviously, you weren't ready to win the tournament."

"What do you mean I wasn't ready? I did everything you said. I focused on the good. I got into the joy of tennis and watched my thoughts. I was mindful of my body and tried to stay in the moment."

"You are a long way down the path, but you haven't reached the destination yet," he said emphatically. "You did everything except one thing."

"What's that?"

"You haven't come to terms with your intentions. You are getting deeper, but you haven't reached the core processor yet. You haven't rewritten the machine language."

"But I have good intentions. I'm not trying to hurt anyone."

"There is no doubt you are a good person, but you haven't convinced yourself of that. And you are not yet speaking the language of intentions. You are skirting around the topic, but you haven't dived in."

"So what are my intentions?"

"You tell me."

"Okay, okay. I still want to win and beat the other guy. I still want to be on top and get adulation. I admit it. Does that make you happy?"

"Actually it does make me happy because you are finally being honest with yourself. One of the worst things in the world is self-deception."

"How do people deceive themselves? That doesn't sound possible."

"It is very common. We deceive ourselves by not acknowledging our true intentions. We work really hard to hide our true intentions from other people, and we do that by denying them to ourselves."

"So you think I have the wrong intentions?"

"They are not wrong per se. They are just scripted by your ego. In effect, your ego is the programmer of your core processor's machine language. This processor is coded to seek status, adulation, and accumulation. Unfortunately, this machine language leads to aggression, envy, disappointment, grasping, and aversion—all of which leads to suffering and unhappiness, for you and the people around you."

"Wow, that sucks. What a mess. But what about the guy who won the tournament? Didn't he have the same bad intentions as me? I keep thinking I wasn't aggressive enough: That I didn't want it enough. And that's why I lost."

"Maybe. But the thing is, if you had won the tournament in your present state, you might still have a problem. Sure, you would have won, but your ego would have won it. You would feel a certain amount of elation for a certain amount of time, but it would be fleeting. Within no time, the joy of victory would be eclipsed by the ego's incessant demand for more. You would then seek another level to conquer, and then another level, and then another level."

"But isn't that the point: To keep striving higher and higher?"

"I'm going to grant that striving and wanting are natural instincts of human beings. But that still brings us back to intentions. What do you really want to strive for?

"I don't know. What do you think I should strive for?"

"Instead of striving for success, fame, and fortune, you could strive for fulfillment, connection, and wholeness. Strive to master yourself, your thoughts, your feelings, and your intentions."

"That's interesting. I've been taught all my life to strive for success. But you are talking about a different kind of success."

"Yes, instead of striving for external success, strive for internal success."

"What is internal success?"

"You can have all of the external forms of success—fame and fortune—and yet have internal failure. You can win all of the tennis tournaments in the world and still feel unfulfilled, disconnected, lonely, confused, and bitter. Internal success means your mind and soul are at peace. You are comfortable with who you are, what you believe in, and what you are doing with your life. You feel relaxed and content."

"That's definitely what I want. Internal success. How do I get it? No one has ever taught me that, especially on the tennis court."

"Yes, it's hard, especially in our culture."

"Why is that?"

"Our core machine language has been programmed for us by our culture because achieving outward material success is our culture's project."

"What do you mean our culture's project?"

"Anthropologists say that every culture has an overall project. It is the defining project that everyone in the society is working on, or at least, is expected to work on. The interesting thing is that most people in the culture do not know it is a project, they just think that is the way it is. So in our western culture, the project is to achieve happiness by amassing material wealth, and most people never question it, or seek another way."

"I can't argue with that. But what are you saying? That our culture's project is wrong?"

"It's not necessarily wrong. It just might not be the project you really want to work on. It might not be good for you. The key is to take a step back and notice what the culture is telling you to do, and then ask yourself if you want to do that."

"You're telling me to be counter-culture, is that it?"

"Not necessarily. I want you to have a choice. If you step back and see what the culture is asking you to do, then you can decide if you want to do it. I learned years ago that I didn't need to fall in lock step with the culture. I could instead think of our culture as a package of suggestions, which I could take or leave."

"So you see our culture as a bunch of suggestions?"

"That's right. You don't have to do everything that your culture is suggesting. You can accept some of the things, and you can pass on other things. You can build your own personal cultural project, so to speak."

"Kind of like a buffet, rather than a fixed menu."

"That's a great analogy. Our culture is like a buffet. You can load up your plate with what you want, and pass on the rest. You don't have to eat everything."

"Okay, I love that. But what does this have to do with tennis again?"

"You are an ambitious, hard-working person, Bill, and that's very laudable. But now you can decide how you want to apply this ambition energy. Do you want to work hard at making your ego happy by accumulating and climbing higher on the ladder of life, or do you want to work hard at being truly happy?"

"I want to be truly happy."

"Do you want to focus on external or internal happiness?"

"When you put it that way, I guess I want to have internal happiness. That makes more sense to me now."

"Then tennis is a great way to work on it. By playing the game, you are putting yourself in situations that test your intentions. When you win and lose points, your ego is going to come jumping in. You can then choose which path to take. Follow the ego, or take a different path. And the wonderful thing is: The more matches you play, the more opportunity you have to work on your personal-culture project."

"Right. Now I have a completely different reason to play tennis.

Instead of just trying to win, I can work on mastering my thoughts and feelings, and stop the ego from controlling my life."

"Now you're getting it."

"I realize three things: One, catering to the ego is a vicious circle that will never make me happy. Two, following my ego doesn't even work. My ego raised the stakes so high that I lost two finals in a row. And three, I can never actually ever win the ego's game. No matter how many tournaments I win, my ego will never be satisfied. Now I understand why I don't want my ego to be my tennis coach anymore."

"That's great. So the next step is to truly address your intentions, and rewrite your core machine language."

"How do we do that?"

"We are going to take a look at your model and anti-model."

"What's that?"

"Let's schedule our next lesson, and we will talk about it all then."

CHAPTER 17
THE LAST GOAL

Three weeks later, I met Coach Conrad for my next lesson, this time under the bubble at his club. He was in a great mood, laughing and smiling with everyone around him. I thought of him as a happy mountain, joyful and yet grounded. I wanted to be like him.

But I was far from being like Coach Conrad at that moment. I was fatigued and stressed. I was caught up in a relationship problem with one of my business associates. I couldn't stop thinking about him and what he had done. I felt betrayed and angry, and I was taking out my frustration on the people nearest and dearest to me.

I also felt confused about what to do, and how to deal with my feelings about what was going on in my life. It seemed impossible that I would ever become a happy mountain. But at least I was out on the court, ready for another mind-bending lesson from Coach Conrad.

"You're not looking so good today," Conrad said softly to me as I pulled my racquet out of my bag.

"Yeah. I'm having a hard time these days. I've got a few things going on in my life that are bothering me," I confessed.

"Can you tell me about it? Do you mind?"

Not at all, I said, and proceeded to relate my story of anger and betrayal. Coach Conrad listened intently, and then asked me: "What kind of person do you really want to be?"

"I know that I don't want to be the way I feel right now. I don't want to feel anger and resentment all the time. I want to feel happy and contented, like you."

I didn't understand what this line of questioning had to do with tennis. It seemed like a therapy session to me. But, like always, I gave Conrad the benefit of the doubt. I knew he was leading up to something important.

"I asked you what kind of person you want to be because I want to help you clarify your model."

"What do you mean, my model?"

"We all have an image or idea in our mind about what kind of person we want to be. I call that your model. We also have an anti-model. The anti-model is the kind of person we don't want to be."

"So we have a model and an anti-model."

"That's right. Everyone has a model and an anti-model."

"I've never heard of that before."

"Most people are not aware that they have a model or an anti-model, but we couldn't function without them. Every time we make a decision, we access our model and our anti-model. The problem is, most people are not aware they have these two mental constructs. They exist, but they are accessed unconsciously."

"Kind of like the machine language you talk about."

"The machine language is your deepest intentions. The model and anti-model are written on top of the machine language. But the similarity is that most people do not know this internal programming exists. And yet everything we do is based on it."

"So what is the model and anti-model again?"

"The model is what we believe is the right way to be, and the anti-model is what we believe is the wrong way to be. For example, you might say that being healthy and fit is part of your model, and being overweight and out of shape is part of your anti-model."

"Yes, that's true. I believe that for myself."

"Right, so you make decisions in your life based on that. You get exercise, play tennis, and eat right."

"Sometimes I get lazy and don't exercise, and maybe pig out on junk food."

"Sure, you're not perfect. You will never achieve your model perfectly, but it does give you guidance and direction. When you pig out on junk food you know that is your anti-model, and you make an effort to eat better after that, based on your model."

"That makes sense. So what has this got to do with what is happening in my life right now, and with tennis?"

"Clarifying your model and anti-model is very useful. Instead of using them unconsciously, you can be deliberate about it, and strengthen your use of them. This will give you more direction and right intention in your life. It will also help you mature more quickly."

"How will it do that?"

"When we have a clearly articulated model and anti-model, it's easier to identify and practice habits that move you towards your model and away from your anti-model. You are more deliberate about it. This builds character and maturity."

"That makes sense."

"Most important, the model approach helps liberate you from the clutches of your ego, both on and off the court. Focusing on goals feeds your ego because it is designed to achieve goals by pursuing status and material success. It continuously chases after trophies, literally and figuratively. In other words, by focusing on goals exclusively, you strengthen your ego and the hold it has on you."

"So achieving goals is a bad thing?"

"Not necessarily. But you have to be careful with goals. The problem is that the attainment of goals is always in the future. When you strive to achieve a goal, your mind is focused on the future, not the present.

"Second, goals don't always reflect your true values. You may be pursuing goals for the sake of other people, or because your culture is telling you to. That's the cultural project I talked about.

"And third, the goal approach often makes us confused and stressed because we might pursue conflicting goals at the same time. For example, we might want to feel more connected to the people at work, while at the same time trying to beat them out for a better job. Or we might want to have more downtime and more leisure, but we also want to make more money, so we work long hours and never take a break."

"I've never thought about it that way before. I always figured goals were a good thing."

"There is nothing wrong with pursuing a goal, but you can be more mindful about them. Otherwise, your goals and your ego might take over. You might pursue a goal that is contrary to your true intentions. For example, you might want to be a good person, but the pursuit of a goal might turn you into a greedy, self-centered person."

"I've gone down that road. I've been obsessed with winning the tournament, and it makes me feel kind of nasty. It makes me feel frustrated, angry, and jealous, and I don't want to be that kind of person. The question is: How can I win the tournament without getting obsessed with that goal?"

"You can put the emphasis instead on achieving your model. Instead of striving towards a specific goal, like winning a tournament, you can strive to realize your model and move away from your anti-model. Or another way of putting it, instead of making it your intention to win the tournament, you can make it your intention to move closer and closer to your model."

"So how do I clarify my model?"

"Tell me what kind of person you want to be, primarily on the tennis court, for now."

"I want to be energetic and yet calm. I want to be mindful of what is going on during each point and use wise shot selection. I want to come to the net and not be afraid of missing a volley. I want to hit my second serve harder, and think through my strategy.

I also want to be a good sport and take the ups and downs of the match in stride."

"That's excellent. You see, you already have a model; we just clarified it by putting it into words. Now I ask you, what is your anti-model, what do you not want to be on the tennis court?"

"I don't want to be a jerk. I don't want to get mad and throw my racquet when I miss a shot, or question my opponent's calls. I don't want to push the ball, or be afraid to come to the net. I don't want to be overly aggressive or let my ego run my tennis game. I also don't want to feel depressed or deflated when I get behind or blow a lead."

"That's really good. So now you have a clear model of who you want to be on the court, and an anti-model—who you don't want to be on the court."

"Yes, that's helpful. But why is it better than just focusing on my goal to beat the other guy?"

"Using models is more effective than using goals, for a number of reasons. First, your model always reflects your values, so it is much more authentic. Unlike a goal, there can be no doubt that your model is something you really want to be. That means you are more likely to stay on track towards being that model.

"Second, while goals focus your mind on the future, models focus you on the present. At any moment, you can assess whether you are following your model or your anti-model, and adjust accordingly. This keeps you grounded in the here and now, which is excellent for enhancing your performance on the court.

"Third, there is no frustration and confusion. We never expect to achieve our model 100 per cent, so there is no need to get down on ourselves or feel that we have failed. Even when we do something that is more anti-model than model, we can always pick ourselves up and start again. And most important, your model is completely integrated. Unlike goals, which can be conflicting, your model is always one cohesive whole. That's why people who use the model approach feel calmer and more relaxed; their entire being is moving towards something wholesome, rather than something disconnected and fragmented."

"So how do I work with my model and anti-model on the tennis court?"

"I suggest you make a list of your model and another list of your anti-model. Then when you are out on the tennis court, make it your objective to be your model."

"So instead of making it my goal to beat the guy, I will make it my intention to embody my model as much as possible."

"Embody is a good word for it. And that's another great thing about the model approach. When you pursue a goal, it is mostly in your head. But when you focus on your model, it's in your body, not just your mind. That's another reason why a model is better; it unites mind and body, and once again that is very useful when you are playing tennis."

"Okay, I'll give it a try."

I did as Coach Conrad recommended. That evening, I wrote down my model and my anti-model. I wanted to be calmer and more mentally steady in a match. I wanted to come to the net more and hit volleys with more confidence. I wanted to place the ball deeper and hit my second serves harder. I wanted to use appropriate shot selection, and think about my strategy before each point. I also wanted to keep my eye on the ball, and move my feet.

For my anti-model, I wrote that I didn't want to be a passive pusher. I didn't want to take myself too seriously, or get mad when I missed a point. I also didn't want to hit my second serves lightly or worry about double faulting. I didn't want to feel frustrated or angry on the court, or get into vertical relating.

Doing the exercise had a very powerful effect on me. While I was doing it, I felt calmer and more serene. It gave me a sense of confidence, and made me feel less confused about things.

I also realized that nothing could stop me from working on my model. There was no way I could fail. No one could take my model away from me, or impede my intention to realize it. I also didn't feel any pressure because I knew I would never achieve my model perfectly. It would always be a work in progress.

In my next game with a good friend of mine, I brought my model and anti-model out on the court. Beforehand, I read over my two lists, and highlighted a few of the key things. I would use appropriate shot selection and stay calm. I would also not be a pusher and not worry about double-faulting.

I had a great time in the match. I kept reminding myself of my model and my anti-model. After each point, I scored myself from 1 to 10, with 1 being the anti-model and 10 being the model. That was fun. As the match wore on, my model/anti-model score got higher and higher. I could feel the whole experience in my body, not just in my head.

I felt looser and more relaxed. I didn't really care what the real score was. It seemed secondary. But the irony was: I won handily 6-1, 6-3. We both played well, but I had the edge. My friend said: "You were hitting your balls deep and more confidently tonight. I was on the defensive the whole time."

I thanked him for his compliment, and praised his efforts as well. He didn't know it, but I was feeling very excited. This was the breakthrough I had been waiting for. I no longer had the intention to beat my opponent. I had the intention to realize my model and move away from my anti-model. Walking off the court, I felt like a happy mountain.

CHAPTER 18
GOING TO THE NET

Working with my model and anti-model was very helpful, both on and off the court. I was clearer about who I wanted to be, and who I didn't want to be. When I played a match, I noticed when I veered towards my anti-model, and could make a quick course correction. I practiced being less judgmental about my lapses, and more forgiving of others.

That was not easy, but I noticed it made me feel better. Jumping all over myself and others for their transgressions made me feel bad, so I vowed to let things go. After all, no one is perfect. We are all trying to make our way in the world, and sometimes it's not easy to do the right thing.

So Conrad's idea about the model and anti-model was extremely helpful. Yet it wasn't the whole answer. I still had a lot of issues. In fact, all of this self-discovery made me even more aware of my shortcomings on the tennis court. I saw more clearly my fear of going to the net. When I ventured to the net, I felt an intense constriction in my chest, and more often than not, I missed my volley. Better to stay back at the baseline, I told myself, it's dangerous up at the net.

I also felt frustrated and defeated when I lost. I never let it show, but I was often crushed by a loss, especially if it was close. It was much more than just a tennis game. The loss felt like a personal defeat, a reflection of a larger disappointment in my life. I had a lot more perspective, and could shrug it off faster, but I did notice that deep down I still felt the sting of a loss and disappointment on a very personal level.

Moreover, I also noticed my feelings of disconnection. Locked in combat, I felt disconnected from my opponents. I tried to invoke Conrad's notion of connection with everything, but it didn't seem authentic to me. Depending on the circumstances, I felt hurt, mistreated, envious, lonely, and inadequate.

They were strong feelings. It was like I was breaking out in a rash all over my body, but this was more like an inner rash. I thought all of my work with Conrad would make me feel better: But it was making me feel worse.

I took my complaint to Coach Conrad: "I thought our work together would make me feel better, but it is making me feel worse. I wish I had never started down this road."

"That's a very common observation," Conrad said. "And it's true. It does actually feel worse just before it feels better. Human beings are naturally averse to feeling pain. So when we start to feel inner pain, we rush in to stop it. That's why people become addicted to drugs and alcohol or lose themselves in work or shopping. They do these things to avoid feeling their deepest wounds. It's called self-medicating."

"Have I been self-medicating?"

"It would be very surprising if you haven't been. You might not be hooked on drugs or anything like that, but you might be hooked on over-working at the office, or trying to make yourself feel better by beating people at tennis."

"Okay. You've got my number. I'm self-medicating."

"Don't worry, just about everybody does it in some way. It's natural to try and suppress pain. But it is not the best idea to do it, because if you self-medicate, the pain will never go away."

"Why is that?"

"Self-medication just dulls the pain, it doesn't get to the heart of it. It doesn't heal it."

"So what do you do to really heal the pain?"

"You have to let it fully express itself. You have to acknowledge it and truly feel the full extent of it. And then it will pass away."

"So it's possible to truly heal your deepest, most intense personal pain?"

"That's the whole point of this work. We are trying to heal your pain so you can fully enjoy life; to liberate yourself from the pain that is stopping you from living life fully."

"You're saying that it's okay that I'm feeling all of these emotions."

"That's right. How you are feeling right now is a good sign. You are finally starting to feel your pain: the pain you have been suppressing all of your life."

"So what's at the heart of it all? What's my deepest pain?"

"That will be for you to discover. But you are getting close. You are reaching the ultimate showdown with your demons. The key is to keep going. Don't turn back now. Your wound will only be healed if you enter the dark chamber and slay the dragon."

"What's the dragon?"

"It's a metaphor. Life is asking you to be a hero in your own life, to summon up your courage and stand face to face with your greatest fear."

"How do I do that?"

"Playing tennis is a great way. Think of it as the battlefield, and you are fighting for your life. But not your physical life, your spiritual life."

"Are you getting all religious on me now?"

"By spiritual I mean your inner life. That's how tennis can help you. By engaging in a battle on the tennis court, it will force you to confront your inner demons. In my opinion, if you want to win the tournament, you have to win this spiritual battle first."

"I totally agree with you on that one. I know I have the physical ability to win. What I need is the inner ability as well."

"That's good. You are getting it."

"So what's the next step?"

"It's important to know about how the mind works on a physical level. This understanding will help you make sense of your emotions, and get to the root of your inner wound."

"So how does the mind work?"

"Over millions of years, the mind has evolved. There are actually three parts of the brain that are designed to meet three core needs: safety, satisfaction, and connection. The safety part of our brain wants to avoid harm. The satisfaction part of our brain wants to get rewards. And the connection part of our brain seeks to attach itself to others."

"What parts of the brain are you talking about?"

"The safety system is attached to the brain stem, which is the old part of the brain. The satisfaction/reward system is connected to the sub-cortex, and the connection/attachment system is linked to the cortex. Each part of the brain evolved one after the other."

"So the safety system in the brain stem is the oldest part of the brain?"

"That's right. That's why the safety instinct is the strongest, most powerful instinct we have."

"Why is it so powerful?"

"Think about it. When human beings were hunters and gatherers, it was very important to keep an eye out for danger. If you let your guard down, you might be eaten by a tiger. So the humans who survived were the ones who were good at staying safe."

"But that was a long time ago."

"That's right. But our brains are still wired for safety, so even when we are on the tennis court, we are more likely to think safety first."

"But what about going to the net?"

"That's about approaching rewards, the second level of the brain. But that is more difficult for most people. If we think about the hunters and gatherers again, you can see why. The humans who were tuned to safety may not have caught the big elephant, but they stayed alive. The humans who focused on chasing the big elephants often took their eye off the ball and got eaten by the tiger."

"So that's why most people would rather stay safe than chase after the big elephant."

"Yes. It is actually wired into our brain. Most people would rather stay at the baseline and push the ball, rather than come to the net and make the point. They are choosing safety over reward."

"So what about connection? You said that is the third part of the brain."

"This is where it gets interesting. Most people long for connection, but they feel disconnected and separate. This is why a lot of people feel lonely, even when they are surrounded by other people."

"Why is that?"

"You can blame the ego for that. When we are striving to stay safe, we can see others as a threat. And when we seek reward, we can see others as an obstacle or a competitor who is seeking the same reward. When we are caught up in either fear or greed, we feel disconnected."

"I feel that way sometimes on the tennis court. I bounce back and forth between fear and greed. When I lose an important point or game I start to fear losing. I tell myself a fear story, envisioning my inevitable defeat. And then I hit a few great shots, and I get all caught up in greed. I tell myself a greed story and envision winning the match and the whole tournament. Sometimes I switch between these two modes in the blink of an eye."

"And how do you feel about the other player at that point?"

"If I'm caught up in fear, I see them as a threat, and if I'm caught up in greed, then I see them as an obstacle."

"Do you feel connected to them?"

"No. They are just this person on the other side of the net."

"And how does that make you feel?"

"I don't know. I guess it feels bad. You're right about one thing. What I want more than anything is to feel connected."

"Tell me more about that."

"You know, I really want to succeed in life, and win things like the tournament, but I get my real happiness by feeling connected to other people, like my friends and family. I also want to feel connected to nature, and to the universe. I know it sounds corny, but that's what I really want."

"Okay, so this is important. You are telling me that feeling connected is more important to you than winning the tournament or staying safe."

"That's right."

"So how are you doing in that game?"

"Not very well. Most of the time, I feel disconnected."

"And how does that make you feel."

"Kind of sick at heart, actually."

"So is tennis helping you with that, or making it worse?"

"I think it's making it worse. Because I'm so focused on

winning, I see people as threats and obstacles and that makes me feel disconnected."

"Can you see the paradox there?"

"What do you mean?"

"You have two conflicting desires: one is to win the tournament, and the other is to feel connected. But if you focus too hard on winning, you feel more and more disconnected."

"How is that a paradox?"

"Because there is another side to that coin. Some people think connection will stop them from winning."

"Why is that?"

"The notion is that connection makes you weak. If you focus on other people, then you will stop striving for reward, and they will win instead."

"Yes, I can see that."

"So that's why it is a paradox. You think: If I focus on winning the tournament, I will lose connection, and if I focus on connection, I won't win the tournament. That's why you had your initial underlying assumption: If I try to win, I am a bad person."

"Oh yes, my underlying assumption. But I'm over that now."

"I'm not sure you are. You are working on it. But I think it's the reason why you keep losing in the finals. You are caught in an endless loop: thinking you can either win or be connected, but you can't have both.

"That's why we should go back to your new underlying assumption: 'I can try to win and still be a good person.'"

"Yes. I remember that. That's how I got started on the psychology of tennis."

"It is the key to the whole thing. You need to go back to using your new rule on the tennis court."

"It worked great until I came up against that guy who beat me 6-0, 6-0."

"It's not only about winning. Remember you can play the best match of your life and still lose because the guy is just better than you. So that's not the objective. The objective is to feel good about what you are doing. To extricate yourself from the dictates of your ego, and realize that no matter what, you are a good person, win, lose, or draw. Nothing that happens on the tennis court can change that."

"So you're saying that I'm a good person no matter what."

"That's right."

"But what if I do something horrible, like hurt someone?"

"That would be wrong, but it would not change the fact that on a fundamental level, you are a good person. It is your ego that gets you in trouble, not your true self."

"That's very positive. I guess I just have a hard time believing it."

"Our ego is very crafty. It boasts and blusters, and tries to pump itself up, but because it is insecure, it tells us lies about our true self. The ego does not want us to give it up, so it tries to convince us that we need it. It tells us that we are a bad person deep down and we need it—the ego—to keep us on track."

"So it's the ego that is telling me I'm a bad person."

"Yes. Your ego tries to undermine your opinion of your true self so that you won't abandon it. That's why many people feel guilty and lack self-esteem and positive self-regard; they take their counsel from their ego. And that's why working on a new underlying assumption—I can try to win and still be a good person—is so powerful. It will help you rewire your brain to see reality more clearly."

"And what is that reality again?"

"Your true self is truly good. Nothing can take that away from you. It is not affected by any conditions, external or internal."

"So I can try to win and be a good person no matter what."

"As long as you have the right intentions."

"What intentions?"

"To focus on connection, rather than reward or fear."

"Right."

"So you could say: 'I can try to win and still be connected.'"

"That's much better. That way, the two things I want are integrated, trying to win and being connected. That's great because I can see now that trying to win so much was making me feel disconnected. I had one foot on the accelerator and another foot on the brake. My unspoken assumption was that if I won the tournament, I would become completely disconnected from everyone, and I didn't want that. So I didn't push through to victory."

"You are really getting it."

"That's also why I don't go to the net very often. I'm actually a net player, not a baseliner. But I don't go to the net because deep down I don't want to win. And I don't want to win because I think that will make me a bad person and I will lose connection."

"That's a great insight."

"Does everyone have this problem?"

"They don't have exactly the same problem. Everyone is unique. But it is very common that people have something blocking them psychologically on the tennis court, and in their life. The key is to be mindful of your thoughts and feelings when you are playing tennis, and then investigate further what might be the underlying reasons why you are having those thoughts and feelings."

"What if you don't like what you discover?"

"Mindfulness is like one insult after another. When you wake up, you realize what you have been doing at the behest of your ego, and that can be startling and unsettling. But soon you realize that the initial shock and pain is worth it. You end up feeling so much better, and you are able to live a much better life, both on and off the court."

"So what should I do in my next match?"

"I want you to try two things. One, keep repeating: I can try to win and still be connected. Two, whenever you have the chance, go the net. Seek the rewards and opportunities that you can only get at the net."

"I can't wait to try it."

CHAPTER 19
GETTING CONNECTED

Next up was a regional tournament. While I played primarily on clay, this tournament was on hard courts, which meant the game would be a lot faster. I knew that going to the net was the perfect strategy for this kind of court. Instead of engaging in long rallies, I would bring my game to the net whenever I had the chance. I would also use my new mantra: I can try to win and still be connected.

In the first round, I came up against Blake. I had lost to him a year earlier, but it had been a close match. I remember that he was a steady baseliner. He also had a hard serve. I won the toss and elected to serve.

On the first point, I decided to rush the net on my service. I thought he would be surprised, but when I arrived at the net, Blake's return had already sailed past my backhand. *Okay, maybe that was a bit premature*, I thought to myself.

On the second point, I took my time and constructed the point. After a short rally, Blake hit me a short ball, which I hit on an angle to his backhand, and charged to the net. Blake's return shot went into the net. 15-all.

Throughout the first set I felt increasingly more comfortable and relaxed. My primary goal was not to win the match. It was to work on coming to the net. I decided I would rather lose by coming to the net than win by rallying from the baseline. That made me feel good. I had nothing to lose.

I didn't go the net on every point because that would be too predictable. I also tried to make sure I only went to the net when appropriate, usually on a short ball. And I tried to hit a decent approach shot that put Blake on the defensive.

The strategy worked great. I was in control of the match, and felt relaxed. I didn't feel any big fear at the net. It felt good to be proactive rather than reactive. I also realized I didn't always have to hit a winning volley at the net. Half the time, Blake hit his attempted passing shot either into the net or out.

But that was just half the story. I was also telling myself: You can try to win and still be connected. That was also working. I felt empowered to go for it and win the match. It was obvious to me that trying to win did not mean I was a bad person, or that it would disconnect me from others. In fact, the opposite was true. The more I focused on my feelings of connection, the better I played, and the more points I won. Focusing on connection was making me a better tennis player. It was all helping me win.

During the match, and upon reflection afterwards, I expanded my definition of connection. Sure, I felt more connected to Blake, although I didn't know him very well, but I also felt more connected to the whole experience. I didn't feel disembodied, I felt more embodied. My body felt connected to the court, and to the world around me. I felt more aware of the pull of gravity on my body and on the ball, which made me feel more connected to the

Earth. It all sounds so wacky and strange, I'm sure, but it was truly profound.

This embodied feeling of connection also improved my game. I wasn't lost in my thoughts—ruminating and running stories through my mind—I was simply connected physically to the whole experience. I felt looser, stronger, and more at ease. I had taken my foot off the brake.

Many times during the match, my ego tried to reassert itself. When I won a big point, I would do a fist pump, and think: *Wow, I'm good. I'm great.* And then I would lose a big point at the net, and slump around thinking: *I suck. What am I doing? I don't belong at the net. It's not safe up there.*

But then I would catch myself. *Hold on, ego,* I'd say to myself. *You're not the boss of me. I'm not going to let you order me around anymore. Back to connection. Back to: I can try to win and still be connected.*

And that was all it took. The ego retreated. I realized it wasn't as strong as I'd thought. It was like a paper tiger.

Interestingly, I ended up losing the match. After I won the first set 6-2, Blake changed his strategy and starting coming to the net too. Now that he was on the offensive, I was more on the defensive. But I still managed to get to the net on most points.

However, the final outcome was 2-6, 6-4, 7-6 in Blake's favor. But it didn't matter to me. I felt I had won. I had tried to win and still felt connected. I think Blake was a little surprised by my ebullience walking off the court. I was happier than him.

Thinking about the match the next day, I recalled something Coach Conrad had told me. Previously, when I focused on trying to win, I got caught up in my ego. I was always tethered to my thoughts—bouncing back and forth between wildly optimistic visions of victory, and bleak forebodings of apocalyptic demise. The predominance of these thoughts meant that I had been playing tennis primarily with my head. And my head was disconnected from my body.

That was my insight: My first level of disconnection was between my head and my body. No wonder I felt disconnected from everyone else in the world. My head wasn't even connected to my own body. And that's because my ego was setting the agenda, which was to win. By accepting that agenda, I had put the ego in charge and created the disconnect.

But when I made connection my intention, my ego lost its mandate. The logic of the ego's argument—that connecting will lead to defeat—was proven invalid. In fact, it had now been proven—at least partially—that connection will lead to victory. Not just the normal kind of victory (winning the match), but a bigger, more important victory, which for me meant I felt better about myself and my connection with life. That was a much bigger prize.

I knew that going forward nothing would ever be the same. I knew the ego would keep popping up and trying to get my attention, but I didn't believe in it anymore. My ego musings and machinations were now more amusing than compelling. I knew in my bones that the strategies being suggested by the ego didn't work. They were like drugs. They might make you feel good in the short term, but they make you feel horrible in the long term and then you are a slave to them.

To the best of my ability, I tried to put into words these insights when I had my next lesson with Coach Conrad. He expressed great pleasure with my progress, and reinforced my sentiments.

"You have discovered a simple truth, that you have always been connected. Everyone and everything is connected. But your ego tries to convince you that you are a separate entity. And the more you listen to your ego and do its bidding, the more disconnected you feel. So if feeling connected is what you actually want, then you now have a powerful incentive to disengage from the agenda of the ego."

"That's why tennis is so exciting for me again," I enthused. "It's not just about getting exercise, and hitting a tennis ball, it is about feeling connected and whole. It is about becoming the person I always wanted to be. The more tennis I play, the more liberated I can be from my ego. I can't wait to play in the club tournament this summer. I am fascinated to see what will happen."

"It's going to be interesting," Coach Conrad concurred.

CHAPTER 20
IT'S NOT LONELY AT THE TOP

The next summer, I signed up for the men's club tournament once again. I was seeded first in the draw, and felt very confident. I could only see one obstacle. Seeded second was Jack Vaughan, a tough player. I had beaten him three times, but he had prevailed the last time we played. He was also 20 years younger than me. But I had my head on straight and felt better than I had in my whole life.

I breezed through the early rounds. I embraced my new rule: I can try to win and still be connected. Discovering the rule to be true over and over again, it became more and more believable. It gave me a lot of joy because I didn't feel at cross-purposes.

Coach Conrad also had some advice. "Watch your energy and effort, and then investigate what is going on," he told me. "If you find yourself striving, look deeper into yourself. Be honest about why you are striving. If you find your energy and effort flagging, do the same thing. Why is your energy flagging? Are you losing hope? Are you falling into despair?"

It was excellent advice. I caught myself striving on many occasions. I could sense it in my body. When I was striving, my body felt very tense. I could tell that my ego had taken the reins. Then I would feel my energy and effort drop. I was aware of losing hope and confidence.

When I fell into either extreme state—striving or giving up—I readjusted my attitude, reaffirming my new intention: I can try to win and still be connected. This gave me balance. My feet felt more connected to the ground, and my physical motions were smoother. There was no longer any doubt in my mind that understanding my personal psychology was having a dramatic impact on my performance.

Following a tough three-set win in the semi-finals against a guy named Derek, who had greatly improved over the previous year, I was once again slated for the finals. Sure enough, I was matched up against Jack Vaughan, who had made it to the finals without losing a set.

Around the club, people were starting to notice that I was in the finals for the third year in a row. Several people made comments about it: "When are you going to win that tournament?" "You better not choke this year, you might not get another chance." "It's three strikes and you're out, Bill." These barbs stung a little, but they didn't bother me too much. I had my secret weapons, and I was radically motivated.

Come finals day, I arrived early at the club. The weather was ideal: Sunny, warm with a slight breeze. There would be no weather factors at play this time. Walking out to the court I had butterflies in my gut, and felt a little shaky in my knees. Jack was looking chipper and well rested. Like me, he had a coterie of supporters on hand to cheer him on.

During the warm-up I kept repeating my new rule, and checking in with my mind and body. My ego tried to tell me a story about losing three finals in a row. After hitting a couple of great practice volleys I also caught myself pursuing a grandiose story of imagined victory. But these thoughts were mere figments of my imagination, and easily swatted away.

One thing I did know: I had a huge advantage over Jack. He didn't know this match was the culmination of 45 years of tennis. He didn't know it was the apogee of my work with Coach Conrad; not only was I trying to win on a physical level, I was also trying to win on a psychological level.

I didn't let myself down. I was totally psyched for every point. I wasn't going to give Jack even the slightest chance of beating me. I played every point like it was my last. I kept feeling the ground under my feet and the ball in my hand. I came to the net repeatedly, forcing the issue, and finishing my volleys. Whenever a story popped into my mind, I ignored it, and it vanished. I stayed tuned into my body, and reaffirmed continuously my intention to try and win and still be connected.

The outcome of the match was never in question. Jack didn't stand a chance. I walked away with a 6-1, 6-2 win in less than an hour. My supporters were ecstatic. They knew how much it meant to me.

Finally I had won a tournament. I had the runner-up monkey off my back. But more important, I had emerged victorious in the right way. I had won and still felt connected. It didn't feel lonely at the top.

A week later, I thanked Coach Conrad for all of his help.

"I'm so happy for you, Bill," he said. "You worked really hard, both physically and mentally to win. Especially as a 52-year-old against a 30-year-old."

"There are some advantages to getting older," I said. "Your body slows down, but you have more insight and personal awareness. That can give you a great advantage on the court."

"Getting older also gives you the chance to strip off the armor of your ego," he added. "You learn that you don't need your ego anymore. And without this armor, you are able to express who you really are, both on and off the court."

"That's really it," I added. "It felt so good to win, because I won, not my ego. I didn't get that sick feeling I used to have, and I didn't feel let down after the match. It was all good."

"So now we are ready to move on to Phase Two."

"I thought we were all done. I won the tournament."

"That's true, but we have only just gotten started. Time to move on to Phase Two."

"What's Phase Two?"

"You'll see."

CHAPTER 21
PHASE TWO: PLAYING THE TRICKSTER

It was the following spring when I had my next lesson with Coach Conrad. He had spent the winter in Florida teaching at one of the top tennis resorts in the U.S. He was bronzed from head to toe, and looking spritely for a fellow in his 60s.

"I haven't seen you since my great triumph," I said, pulling my racquet from my bag. "I've been very curious about Phase Two. I thought winning the tournament was the end of it, but you said that we had only gotten started."

"That's right. Now it's time for the return."

"What? You mean my return of serve?"

"No. We can work on that too if you want, but I'm talking about the return of the hero."

"What hero?"

"You. You are the hero. You embarked on your quest, and slayed the dragon. You must now return from your adventure, and share what you have learned."

"You want me to share what I learned?"

"That's right."

"But I don't want to. Then other people will know the secret and they will beat me. I want to keep it all to myself."

"Sounds like your ego is the one that returned, Bill."

"What do you mean?"

"The one thing you learned was that you can try to win and still be connected. It doesn't sound like you want to be connected anymore."

"No. I want to be connected."

"Then the best way to be connected is to share with others what you have learned on the tennis court."

"I guess you're right. But how do I teach other people what I've learned. I'm not a guru like you."

"You can teach people by playing the trickster."

"What's a trickster?"

"In mythology, the trickster is a character that uses tricks and other antics to shake people up so they can see the world from a different perspective. The trickster helps people see that they are trapped in their ego, by playing harmless pranks on them."

"That's interesting. I guess I've always been a bit of a trickster. I like to shake people out of their ego stupor, that's for sure. But how can I play the trickster on the tennis court? Do you want me to hit drop shots or something?"

"It's sometimes useful to hit tricky shots, but I'm talking about psychology. You can play some mind tricks to make people more aware of their psychology out on the court."

"What kind of mind tricks?"

With that question, Coach Conrad looked around and then bent his head conspiratorially, and laid out a crazy plan for my next match, coming up the following week. It was a wacky plan, but I couldn't wait to set it in motion.

The next week, I arrived early for my match. It was the last regional tournament of the indoor season. My opponent was Trevor, a super fellow I had known for years. We were evenly matched and always had a hoot out on the court. He was the perfect victim for my "trick."

The match progressed as expected. Trevor won the first game on his serve, and I won the second on my serve. I almost broke his serve in the third game, but he held by hitting two aces in a row.

On the changeover, I sat down on the bench, and pulled a piece of paper out of my pocket. I studied it very intently and then put it back in my pocket. I saw out of the corner of my eye that Trevor was watching me scrutinize the piece of paper.

I won the next game on my serve, and then broke Trevor's serve in the fifth game. I was now up 3-2. On the changeover, I once again pulled out the piece of paper and stared at it intently. I saw Trevor glance over and then stare at the ground.

And so it went. On each changeover, I pulled out the piece of paper and looked at it. I didn't make a big show of it, but I could see that Trevor was definitely intrigued—so much so that his game started to unravel. He double faulted a few times, and missed some easy points at the net, usually his strong suit. After winning the first set 6-4, I easily took the second set 6-1.

As he came to the net at the end of the match, Trevor had a twisted, perplexed look on his face. "Hey, congratulations, Bill, but what the heck was that piece of paper all about? What did you write on it?"

I smiled puckishly and pulled the paper out of my pocket. "Nothing, Trevor, there was absolutely nothing written on it."

"What do you mean, nothing?" Trevor exclaimed in exasperation. "Why would you do that?"

"There is no rule that says I can't look at a piece of paper on the changeover, is there?"

"Well no. But it seems like a pretty weird thing to do."

"Yeah, but it kind of worked, didn't it?"

"That's for sure. I couldn't think about anything else in the second set. I just kept wondering what in the world you had written on that piece of paper. It completely unnerved me out there."

"Why do you think it unnerved you?" I asked, warming up to my trickster role.

"I couldn't think about anything else. I figured you had some awesome new strategy. When you won a point, I tried to think what strategy you used, but I couldn't think of anything. It drove me crazy. Then I got mad. It wasn't fair. You can't look at a piece of paper. It's just not done."

"I had a great time," I retorted. "I could see it was driving you crazy. It was so much fun."

For the next hour in the lounge, I told Trevor all about my lessons with Coach Conrad, and how I had overcome my psychological issues to win the tournament. Trevor didn't completely grasp everything I told him, but he vowed to book a lesson with Coach Conrad.

During the next match, I played my second trick with Nestor, someone whom I had never played before. I loved this trick because it wasn't really a trick at all. After every point that Nestor won, I congratulated him on his play. "Excellent shot. Great volley. That was an amazing backhand. Incredible."

You would think that my laudatory exclamations would have propelled Nestor to a resounding victory, but they seemed to have the opposite effect. As a taciturn gent bent on conquest, Nestor was sent into some kind of mangled mental state by my blandishments. He wanted to hate me, objectify me, but how could he do that to someone who was praising his every shot? He knew he should reciprocate my kind words, but that wasn't part of his game plan. I could see a flash of guilt cross his face whenever I'd make a great shot. *I should say something nice to Bill*, he was no doubt thinking, *but that's not part of my game plan.*

I kept it up right until the end. "Super rally. Incredible lob. Nice serve." I was revoltingly gracious, just brimming with bombastic bonhomie. From across the net, I was tampering with the very circuitry of Nestor's noggin.

At the conclusion of the match, which I won 7-6, 6-3, Nestor ambled to the net and offered me a bemused and confused proffering of congratulations. I could see that he had never experienced anything like our match before. I had shaken up Nestor's world view of life on the tennis court. *What fun*, I thought.

A few weeks later, I played in the ladder at my club down by the lake. Sacha was my victim on this occasion. He was 22 years old and full of youthful cockiness. Every ball was a cannon shot, accompanied by a cacophony of snorts, grunts, and zesty fist-pumps: A perfect opportunity for the trickster to strut his stuff.

Being 53 years old at the time, I was more than twice his age, and this was not lost on Sacha. I knew he considered his situation a no-winner. If he won, then all he had done was beat an old guy. But if he lost, well, then he had lost to an old guy.

I thought I would combine my tactic against Nestor—a steady stream of superlative praise for his prowess—with a new tactic, the slow, slithering shuffle of the elderly. As Sacha pranced about the court, trying to rush from point to point, I took my good time slowly picking up balls from the back of the court. Slow and steady. The molasses march of the aged. Bending over to pick up balls, I placed my palm on my lower back, just in case my geriatric spine were to fail me once and for all. For each serve, I bounced the ball three or four times. I slowed down my service motion. I hit high lumbering lobs. Followed by kindly kudos between points.

I could see that Sacha, like Nestor, was coming apart at the seams. I had deliberately booked court one so his friends could gather around to watch. Sacha kept looking over at his friends every time he missed a shot. He became tense and irascible. He threw his racquet and cursed in Russian. Down, down Sacha went, descending into his own personal hell.

At the end, Sacha was a tangled knot of self-recrimination and self-loathing, having lost the match 8-4 to a guy old enough to be his Dad, in front of his friends, on court one. I felt for Sacha, but as the trickster, I knew I had done him a favor. His ego had taken him out on the court full of bluster and bravado, and now he had to drag his ego off the court in a stretcher.

These experiences taught me why the old and wise often outperform the young and callow. They have made peace with their inner demons, and now understand the landscape of the mind. This insight helps them navigate the world adroitly, skating rings around the young, who are usually trapped, marching to the orders of their ego.

When I thought about Trevor, Nestor, and Sacha, and the tricks I had played on them, I wondered if I was actually playing fair. Was it moral and ethical to use my new psychological insights on them? Was it right to play tricks on them? I hashed this debate around for a while, and came to the conclusion that Conrad was right. It was my role now to help others confront their delusions on the tennis court. Not in a mean and nasty way, but in a humorous and fun way that would shake them up a bit.

I was perturbed, however, to learn that Sacha dropped out of the ladder. He told his friends that playing the ladder was ruining his game because the contestants weren't very good. Too many pushers and old guys, he said derisively. I chuckled at that comment because I knew what old guy he was referring to. I hoped that Sacha would one day realize he had beaten himself, and that winning matches isn't the point of playing tennis.

CHAPTER 22
HEALING THE WOUND

Feeling in great spirits, I booked a tennis lesson with Conrad, and invited him out for dinner afterwards to show my appreciation for everything he had done for me. I was not only playing better tennis and enjoying it more, I was experiencing greater peace of mind in my life. I didn't feel like life was a battle to be won and a long, hard journey to be endured. I didn't feel like I was rolling a ball up a mountain, only to have it come tumbling back down again. I didn't feel fantastic every moment, but my general experience of life was better.

Coming out onto the court, I was struck by Conrad's warmth and general amiability towards the world. He obviously practiced what he preached, and was a great role model. Even in his 60s, after teaching tennis for more than 40 years, he exuded a freshness and curiosity rare even in the youngest.

I told Conrad about my trickster escapades, and he roared with laughter. "That's outstanding," he said. "You're doing a great job shaking people up. Good for you."

"Yes, and it's fun too," I said. "I love to see how they react to my tricks. It's added a whole new element to playing tennis."

"So now we move on to phase three," Conrad said, pulling his racquet out of his bag.

"What's phase three?"

"That's when you pull it all together, and exorcise your wound once and for all."

"But I thought I did that already."

"No. There is actually one more act to this story. You have to arrive at the ultimate insight into your personal psychology."

"What insight is that?"

"That's for you to discover, not for me to tell you. But for now, let's work on some of your tennis strokes. Then when we have dinner, I'll explain phase three to you."

At dinner, I immediately asked Conrad about phase three. "So what's this all about? I thought we were done. I'm a little perturbed that there is more to go."

"Don't worry. This is the good part. You are going to be able to heal your wound once and for all."

"What is my wound?"

"I can't say what yours is, but everyone has one. It is something in our life that has wounded us, usually when we were children, but not necessarily. We can also be wounded as adults."

"Can you give me an example of a wound?"

"Let me start by saying that being human is hard. When we come into this world, we are confronted with many challenges. We are vulnerable to, as Hamlet said, 'the thousand natural shocks that flesh is heir to.' You might experience deprivation by growing up poor. You might be abandoned by your caregivers and feel unloved. You might be born into a large family, and feel insignificant and lost in a crowd. You might feel stupid, or unattractive. You might feel like a failure, or unworthy. You might feel guilty about something, or feel a great sense of shame."

"You think everyone feels these things?"

"Everyone has something, and it's usually a unique mix of things. But it's just natural that we become wounded by something, because life isn't perfect."

"But most people seem pretty together. I get it with a drug addict or a criminal, but do most ordinary, functioning people have a wound, too?"

"That's why tennis is such an interesting activity. When people play tennis, their wound often comes to the surface. It's such a great way to explore your own personal psychology."

"So why are people's wounds not obvious to other people?"

"That's where the ego comes in. People develop an ego self to paper over their wound, and the greater the wound, the thicker the paper."

"Like what?"

"Well, if someone is feeling unworthy, they might put a lot of effort into achieving something, like winning a tournament. If they feel unloved, they might try to get everyone to love them, maybe by letting other people walk all over them. Or if they feel shame, they might act with anger when they lose a point."

"So all of these behaviors are just masks to cover over a wound?"

"That's right."

"So what's wrong with doing that? If it's a wound, isn't it a good idea to use the ego to deal with it?"

"The problem is, it doesn't work. Using the ego to heal your wound is like pouring gasoline over a fire, it just makes it worse."

"Why is that?"

"Well, let's take the first example. Let's say you are trying to reach the top of the tennis ladder because you feel unworthy. You think getting to the top will make you feel worthy and heal your wound. And maybe you do make it to the top. But it doesn't work, because the harder you strive to get to the top, the more obvious it becomes to you, deep down, that you are unworthy."

"Yes, I can see that."

"Moreover, you are also clinging to a solution that won't last because sooner or later someone is going to replace you at the top of the ladder. Then you will be back to feeling unworthy again. It's like taking drugs. They might make you feel good at first, but when they wear off, you feel worse."

"So if it doesn't work, why do we all keep trying to make it work? Why do we use the ego so much, even though it doesn't work?"

"We've been conditioned by our culture to think it works. Everyone is telling us to strive for more: more money, more fame, more beauty. But it's a book of lies. If we think these things will make us happy, then we have been deceived, because all of them are transitory and impermanent. It's like trying to grab the fog, or hold onto a perfect day. It just slips through our fingers."

"That conditioning is very powerful."

"You bet it is. So many people have a stake in perpetuating it too. And the biggest problem is the emphasis on self-esteem."

"Why is self-esteem a problem?"

"For decades, psychologists, teachers, coaches, and the media have been touting the importance of self-esteem. Low self-esteem has been seen as the problem for all kinds of personal and social ills. The way to solve the world's problems, the thinking went, was to enhance everyone's self-esteem."

"But isn't high self-esteem good?"

"It's good on one level to have positive self-regard, but it shouldn't be the main focus."

"Why's that?"

"Because the emphasis on self-esteem is the first chapter in the book of lies. The lie is that having high self-esteem will make us happier and more productive. But that is not necessarily true. In fact, by focusing on high self-esteem, we often end up less happy and less productive."

"How does it make us less happy?"

"When we try to boost our self-esteem, we usually focus on external factors, like winning a tournament or looking good or accumulating money. But if we base our self-esteem on these factors, we usually feel we have fallen short. That's why people rant and rave on the tennis court. They are using tennis to boost their self-esteem, and when they lose a point or a match, they feel shame, and mask it over with anger and self-recrimination. Or worse, they blame something else, like the weather or their sore knee."

"But what if we win the tournament?"

"That's great. But you might not win the tournament next year. And if your self-esteem was based on winning, then you will be back in the dumpster soon enough."

"That makes sense, but how does self-esteem make us less productive?"

"When we are trying to boost our self-esteem, the stakes are very high. Everything is riding on it. So fear enters the game. And fear plays havoc on your performance. You get worried every time you lose a point. You play tentatively because you are afraid of losing. You also make pre-excuses to self-handicap yourself."

"What do you mean by self-handicap yourself?

"It's the reason why people make pre-excuses before the match, or make excuses after the match. Their ego's over-riding need for self-esteem makes them feel shame when they lose, and they can't tolerate the notion that maybe the other guy is a better tennis player, or that they played badly that day. No, there always needs to be an excuse."

"Well, we've all done that."

"Exactly, we've all done it, but only some people start to notice the game they are really playing. And all of these excuses and self-denial don't help us become better tennis players. If we tell ourselves, and others, that we lost because we had a hangover or because we weren't wearing the right tennis shoes, then we don't learn anything. And that's not going to make us a better tennis player."

"So that's why you put so much emphasis on psychology; because it helps us become better tennis players."

"That's right. If we become mindful of our need for self-esteem, then we can unhook ourselves from the ego game. We can then gain insight into our delusions and get to the heart of our motivations and intentions. And this insight leads us to the heart of our wound. And that's where the final battle is waged."

"Why is it a battle?"

"It's a battle because it gives you the final opportunity to wrestle control of your life out of the hands of your ego, so you can finally heal your wound."

"How do I wrestle control of my life away from my ego?"

"You start with self-compassion. Recognize your suffering for what it is, and have compassion for yourself. Instead of giving yourself a hard time for your shortcomings, have compassion for yourself. Accept that you are not perfect, and that you will fail sometimes. Accept that you will never play tennis perfectly, or live life perfectly. Accept that you are human. Accept that you have wounds, and take care of yourself."

"But what is my wound?"

"Let's think back to the start of this story. You said that you let people win matches because you didn't want to feel like a bad person."

"Right, and I created a new rule that I could try to win and still be a good person."

"Then we ultimately changed the rule to 'I can try to win and still be connected.'"

"That was even better, and that's why I finally won the tournament."

"Yes, and it's all good because it points directly to your wound."

"Yes, but what is it?"

"Why do you think you are not a good person? Why do you feel disconnected? What do you think is at the core of these thoughts and feelings?"

"Well, I guess I just want people to like me."

"Why do you want people to like you?"

With these words, I suddenly felt very uneasy, but I pushed through: "Because I don't think I am likeable. I don't think I am lovable."

"There you are. That is your wound. For reasons that may never be fully known, you don't feel you are lovable, because you didn't get the love that you needed at a crucial point in your life."

I could feel some tears welling up in my eyes, but held them back as best I could. I didn't want to start balling my eyes out in a restaurant.

"Don't worry, just have compassion for yourself. It's not that you are unlovable. That's just your ego talking. It's just your deepest conditioning."

At that moment, I had the insight that changed my life: "That's the real game I've been playing. I've been trying to get everyone in the world to like me. That's been my happiness project: Once everyone in the world likes me, then I will be happy."

"So how is that project coming along?"

"Not very well. Obviously not everyone in the world is going to love me. So I am constantly disappointed. Then I get angry when someone looks at me the wrong way. And of course, I'm always looking for examples of how people don't like me."

"And how does that play itself out on the tennis court?"

"When I let people win, I did it so that people would like me. But I also thought people would like me if I won the tournament: That success would make me popular and lovable. These two things were contradictory, so I couldn't decide which way to go. I just froze."

"So how do you feel about all that now?"

"I feel relieved. I can see what I've been doing my whole life. Everything I've been doing has been centered around getting people to like me."

"Because?"

"Because my unconscious wound is that I think I am not worthy of love."

"And what is the truth of that?"

"I've been looking outward for love and acceptance, when I should focus on loving and accepting myself."

"Why is that better?"

"Because I have control over it. It is coming from inside me, not from outside me."

"Anything else?"

"Yes. I realize I've been beating myself up. I've been trying to heal my wound by winning tennis tournaments and getting to the top of the ladder. But it hasn't been working. Striving for these goals, with those intentions, actually makes me feel less worthy and less lovable, even if I achieve them."

"So what can you do now?"

"Now I can focus on taking care of myself, and liking myself first. I don't need other people to like me, certainly not everyone in the world. Then I can enjoy myself out on the tennis court. I can try to win, but not make the stakes so high. In fact, I think I'll have even more energy and enthusiasm because I won't be working so hard. It will just be fun."

Conrad was beaming from ear to ear. Both of us sat together in quiet contemplation. I felt calm and at peace. I savored the soothing tranquility inside me.

EPILOGUE

Tennis has been one of the great blessings of my life. Since I first picked up a wooden Slazinger racquet at the age of eight, I've been enamored with this wonderful game. I love the flow of the ball back and forth, and how it feels when you hit a great shot. I love the whole milieu of the sport, hanging out by the court, hearing the smack of the balls. I love meeting other tennis players, and having a "hit" with them. I think tennis is the best game in the world.

But Coach Conrad taught me that tennis is more than just a game. It's an opportunity to learn about myself. What are my real intentions? What are my real motivations? What is my ego all about? What is my ego compelling me to do that might not be in my best interests? And even more important: Who do I want to be? How do I want to live my life? What is most important to me?

Some of my friends scoffed at this way of thinking. Tennis is just a game, they said. What's with all of this psychology stuff? A few have had a good laugh about my wound. But that is their loss. They are missing the true richness of the tennis experience. They are still caught in the suffering of their ego. And I'm sad to think that they will never heal *their* wound, whatever that might be.

With my new perspective, I can see the suffering people experience out on the tennis court. A lot of players look really sad or upset when they are playing, especially those who are actually pretty good. They mope around the court, and throw a fit. They despair at a missed point and fall into depression. They make pre-excuses and post-excuses. They compare themselves to other players. And yet, when they walk off the court, they say they had a great game. It's strange.

I feel so fortunate to have stepped off the ego treadmill. I'm having more fun. Tennis is just a great time, no matter what happens. Sure, sometimes I get back on the treadmill. I still get angry sometimes when I miss a shot, and get caught up in winning at all costs. But most of the time I catch myself doing it, and stop.

I'm also happy that I achieved my dream of winning a tournament. That was a great experience. It taught me that it's better to win when you have the right intentions. It makes the victory taste even sweeter.

After four years of trying, I also ended up ranked 9th in Ontario for players over 45 years of age. That was really exciting. It was a huge challenge because the competition was fierce. But by striving to achieve this goal, I also learned a lot about myself.

Some of my friends have bought into what I learned from Coach Conrad. Some of them have started to take lessons from him too. They are the most fun to play with, because they have more personal insight, and are willing to share their inner experiences with me. They have learned that tennis is a great opportunity to learn about how their mind works. They have also learned that tennis is a great opportunity to heal their wounds, and achieve their full potential, both on and off the court.

So let's play.

ACKNOWLEDGEMENTS

My tennis universe is ever-expanding, so there are so many people to thank. I will start with my tennis coaches over the years, starting with Don Steele, who got me started in tennis at Davisville Tennis Club in Toronto. Then I learned the finer points of tennis during my teenage years from Derek Bouquet at the Badminton & Racquet Club. The many coaches from around the world at The Inn At Manitou taught me how to be a good tennis instructor, including Peter Burwash, a legendary forward-thinker in the sport. More recently, I got invaluable instruction from Tom Kern, who recently received the award for the top tennis coach in Canada.

On the personal development side, I have to thank Beverly Yates and her husband Jim Bean for their decades-long guidance into the inner reaches of my psyche. What a long strange trip it's been. I would also like to thank Molly Swan and Norman Feldman at True North Insight Meditation Centre.

On the tennis court, I've had the pleasure to play with hundreds of people, too numerous to list here.

This book would never have been born without my wife Ginny. She got the whole thing started in California at the CBT conference. Without her help in coming up with my new rule, I can't imagine where I would be today.

In addition, I appreciate the support of several tennis buddies who read early drafts of the book and gave me useful guidance. They include Gregor Binkley, Scott Colby, Liz Smart, Bill

Buckler, Diana Bishop, Adrian Baldeo, Charlotte DeHeinrich, Don Hogarth, Hope McFall, and Jim Matthews.

I want to thank Nancy Smith and Nona Lupenec for supporting me, and freeing up my time to work on my books and creative projects.

Finally, I'd like to thank those people who helped me with the production of the book, including Lynne Shuttleworth, Sonia Marques, and Corey Kilmartin. Thanks for helping me hit this book over the net and keeping it within the lines.

And of course, I want to thank Coach Conrad. Thank you for teaching me how to win the psychological game of tennis (and life).

WHO IS COACH CONRAD?

The big question is: Who is Coach Conrad? Is he a real person or a figment of the author's imagination? Is he a composite character cobbled together from a variety of different people? Is Conrad his real name or an alias?

Itching to know? Send us an e-mail at **bill_bishop@biginc.com** and all will be revealed.

GOINGTOTHENET.NET

If you want more information about the psychology of tennis, you can visit our website, which is an online companion to this book. You can access these resources to help you by going to **GoingToTheNet.Net**.

As a purchaser of this book, you can access the members-only section by entering the password **whoiscoachconrad?**

BOOKS & USEFUL RESOURCES

Books

Aron, Elaine N., **The Highly Sensitive Person**

Berger, Diane and Lisa, **We Heard the Angels of Madness**

Burford-Mason, Aileen, Ph.D., **Eat Well, Age Better**

Bourne, Edmund J., **The Anxiety & Phobia Workbook**, 3rd ed.

Davis, Martha, **The Relaxation & Stress Reduction Workbook**

Doidge, Norman, **The Brain that Changes Itself**

Frankel, Vicktor, **Man's Search for Meaning**

Gilbert, Paul, **The Compassionate Mind**

Greenberger, Dennis and Christine Padesky, **Mind Over Mood**

Greenspan, Miriam, **Wisdom in the Dark Emotions**

Haidt, Jonathan, **The Happiness Hypothesis**

Kushner, Harold, **When Bad Things Happen to Good People**

Learner, Harriet, **The Dance of Anger**

Miller, Alice, **The Drama of the Gifted Child**

Miller, Alice, **The Body Never Lies**

Moore, Thomas, **Care of the Soul**

Nelson., John E and Andrea, **Sacred Sorrows: Embracing and Transforming Depression**

Peck, Scott M., **The Road Less Traveled**

Real, Terrence, **I Don't Want to Talk About It**

Remen, Rachel Naomi, **Kitchen Table Wisdom: Stories that Heal**

Zuercher-White, Elke, **An End to Panic**

Mindfulness Books and CDs

Bennett-Goleman, Tara, **Emotional Alchemy: How the Mind can Heal the Heart**

Brach, Tara, Radical Acceptance: **Embracing Your Life with the Heart of a Buddha**

Brach, Tara, **True Refuge: Finding Peace and Freedom in Your Own Awakened Heart (2012)**

Chodron, Pema, **When Things Fall Apart**

Chodron, Pema, **Living With Uncertainty**

Chodron, Pema, **Taking the Leap**

Chodron, Pema, **The Pema Chodron Audio Collection (CDs)**

Epstein, Mark, **Going to Pieces without Falling Apart**

Epstein, Mark, **Thoughts Without a Thinker**

Germer, Christopher, **The Mindful Path to Self-Compassion**

Gilbert, Paul, **The Compassionate Mind**

Goldstein, Joseph and Jack Kornfield, **Seeking the Heart of Wisdom**

Goldstein, Joseph, **Mindfulness: A Practical Guide To Awakening**

Gunaratana, Bhante Henepola**, Mindfulness in Plain English**

Hanh, Thich Nhat, **The Heart of the Buddha's Teachings: Transforming Suffering into Peace, Joy, and Liberation**

Hanh, Thich Nhat, **Transformation and Healing**

Hanh, Thich Nhat, **Meditation and Psychotherapy (CDs)**

Hanh, Thich Nhat, **Anger (CDs)**

Hanh, Thich Nhat, **The Present Moment (CDs)**

Hanson, Rick and Richard Mendius, **Buddha's Brain: The Practical Neuroscience of Happiness, Love and Wisdom**

Kabat-Zinn, Jon, **Full Catastrophe Living**

Kabat-Zinn, Jon, **Wherever You Go There You Are**

Kabat-Zinn, Jon, **Coming to Our Senses**

Kabat-Zinn, Jon, **Guided Mindfulness Meditation (CD's)**

Kitchen, Kate et al, **Meditation for Mindfulness (CD set)**

Kornfield, Jack, **A Path With Heart**

Kornfield, Jack, **The Inner Art of Meditation (CD set)**

Kornfield, Jack, **Guided Meditation (CD set)**

Kornfield, Jack, **The Wise Heart (CD set or book)**

Kornfield, Jack, **The Art of Forgiveness, Lovingkindness, and Peace**

Neff, Kristin, **Self-Compassion: Stop Beating Yourself Up and Leave Insecurity Behind**

Orsillo, Susan M and Lizabeth Roemer, **The Mindful Way Through Anxiety**

Rosenberg, Larry, **Breath by Breath: The Liberating Practice of Insight Meditation**

Salsberg, Sharon, **Loving-Kindness: The Revolutionary Art of Happiness**

Siegal, Dan, **The Mindful Brain: Reflections and Attunement in the Cultivation of Well-Being**

Skyes, Lucinda, **Body Scan Meditation (CD)**

Sykes, Lucinda, **Sleep and Deep Relaxation (CD)**

Williams, Mark, John Teasdale, Zindel Segal, and Jon Kabat-Zinn, **The Mindful Way Through Depression (book and CD)**

Websites

dharmaseed.org: Free downloads of Insight Meditation talks and guided meditations in the Buddhist tradition.

mindfulwaythroughanxietybook.com: Free audio downloads of short meditations from The Mindful Way Through Anxiety.

self-compassion.org: Website on Self-Compassion by Kristin Neff.

soundstrue.com: Guided meditations or talks by Tara Brach, Pema Chodron, the Dalai Lama, Joseph Goldstein, Jon Kabat-Zinn, Jack Kornfield, Sharon Salzberg and Thich Nhat Hanh.

tarabrach.com: Website contains videos, text, talks and guided meditations.

themindfulnessclinic.ca: Free downloads of meditations.

wisebrain.org: Website on the interface of meditation and neuroscience by Rick Hanson Ph.D. Contains text, talks and guided meditations.

mindfulmood.com: Website for The Mindful Mood Centre in Toronto founded and operated by Dr. Virginia McFarlane, wife of the author. The Mindful Mood Centre provides workshops on mindfulness.

ABOUT THE AUTHOR

Bill Bishop is a writer, entrepreneur, and life-long tennis enthusiast. He has been playing tennis for more than 50 years. He taught tennis for five years during the 1970s. He is also the founder of Bishop Communications Inc., a successful marketing communications company, with its head office in Toronto, Canada. His company specializes in helping its clients use psychology-based marketing strategies. He is married to Dr. Ginny McFarlane, the founder of **The Mindful Mood Centre** in Toronto. He has two children, Douglas and Robin.

To reach Bill call 647.436.8829 x101
or e-mail: bill_bishop@biginc.com

Made in the USA
Lexington, KY
02 August 2014